Rickshaws to Jets Via Memory Lane

by

Kusum

authorHOUSE®

AuthorHouse™
1663 Liberty Drive, Suite 200
Bloomington, IN 47403
www.authorhouse.com
Phone: 1-800-839-8640

This book is a work of non-fiction. Unless otherwise noted, the author and the publisher make no explicit guarantees as to the accuracy of the information contained in this book and in some cases, names of people and places have been altered to protect their privacy.

First published by AuthorHouse 4/14/2008

ISBN: 978-1-4343-6189-9 (sc)

Library of Congress Control Number: 2008900067
Printed in the United States of America
Bloomington, Indiana

This book is printed on acid-free paper.

This book is dedicated to my Mother, who showed me the way, my Grandmother who sacrificed so much for her family and my Didi (Guari), and Mira.

Forward

Having lived for several years in India I was always curious about the diverse superstitions and customs of its culture which spans some 5000 years or so.

This story, by a young Indian woman who managed to break out of the mould and carved a niche for herself in our Western society has been for me, a fascinating revelation. It enabled me to better appreciate and understand some of the enigmas that still exist and are still practiced in India.

This is a heartwarming account of the pursuit and achievement of goals until recently considered rediciculous to even contemplate. From humble beginnings, rickshaws and bullock carts, to life in the fast lane, Dr. Kusum fulfilled ambitions unheard of mere decades ago to become an internationally recognized and acclaimed female doctor from India.

Her story is refreshingly reported honestly, singularly lacking in ego and arrogance. It is a from-the-heart account of Dr.Kusum's journey from the holy city of Varanasi in India, where she was born and raised, through academia and vastly different social life, to an enviable achievement of dreams and goals that would not –could not- possibly have been contemplated a short lifetime ago.

Life is changing in India, and Dr. Kusum's story enables one to better appreciate and understand some of those changes. Some of the old superstitions and customs are still practiced however, despite current laws of prohibition. Life will surely continue to change in India, and it will take on a new meaning, hopefully sooner than later.

John Lee

THINK

If you think you are beaten, you are. If you think you dare not, you don't.
If you like to win but you think you can't, it is almost certain you won't.
If you think you'll lose, you are lost. For out of the world we find
Success begins with a fellow's will. It's all in the state of mind.
If you think you are outclassed, you are. You got to think high to rise.
You have got to be sure of yourself before you can ever win a prize.
Life's battles don't always go to the stronger or faster man.
But sooner or later the man who wins is the man WHO THINKS HE
CAN

Author Unknown

Prologue

In Kolkata Dec.2005, (Calcutta) while giving a short introductory talk for my aunt's anniversary celebration; it occurred to me to write about all the women who were important in my life, beginning with my grandma, my mother, sisters and friends. This then, is my story about the Indian women in general, comparatively, I will also talk later about my non- Indian friends. Here is what I said then in Kolkata.

Ladies and Gentlemen:

I am delighted to be here to celebrate this anniversary in honor of my aunt, Shanti Rani. She and my mother, Shobha Rani were sisters, and their relationship was very close and unique. They were friends and also confidants. Masi (aunt) was like our mother. Also they were ahead of their times, in dieting and weight control. While Masi ate as little as possible, as she realized she did not need a lot of food to nourish her tiny body and stayed slim, my mother believed in exercise and walked a mile a day to stay healthy. At present, exercise and eat less calories are the mantra for weight loss and health. The two ladies went on to live into their eighties and nineties.

Today, I will talk about their childhood. Two sisters were born in Varanasi to a well- to –do Zamindar (landlord) family. They were two among seven kids. They were very intelligent and good in mathematics and sciences. They were admitted to a girl's school, but one of their cousins, Mr Noni decided that they should not be going to school, because the girl's school was adjacent to a boy's school. According to him it is not good for the girls to travel, though they went in a covered horse drawn carriage, because boys will be looking at them, or the girls may attempt to peep out, and get ideas. He, therefore, advised his uncle, the father of the girls that they be removed from the school. Lo and behold, their father, i.e, my grandfather, a weakling, in my opinion, agreed with Noni and ordered the girls out of the school.

The girls were sad, but too young to protest and stayed home to prepare for marriage in due course. The old ladies in the household stayed silent and quickly accepted the situation. Shanti Rani was proud of her 4th grade certificate, which years later she showed me. While all this was going on, their oldest brother was given every possible help to obtain a D.Sc degree from a city far away from Varanasi. I think, this was happening around the nineteen twenties.

This discrimination is still prevalent , as I quote an article from one of your newspaper, "All is not fair for the girl child in modern homes". In short, parents prefer to wait a few days before taking a girl child to a doctor if she falls sick.

Identically, a boy child will be attended immediately medically.

This suppression of women in every way, including female fetal abortion continues resulting in women shrinking in number in India. This is a country where there are more men than women. A time may come when a woman will keep a harem of men, A la Draupadi (a main female character in an Indian epic, Mahabharata).

Shanti Rani grew up to be a beautiful young lady, and was married at a very early age. Her main achievement was the pro- creation of four good men. She was also very much interested in social work, and helped many people in need. She once gave away her gold jewels to some one very much in need of help. However, I must say the social work that I saw only a few days ago, here in Kolkata by a German lady, makes me think that Indian women do not let their potentials come to full fruition. Perhaps they do not have the vision or enough family support.

Here, I would like to compare the life of a little girl who grew up quite a few decades before my aunt was growing up. Her name was Maria Butroskaya, born in Poland in 1867 in a not so well- to- do family, in a country not as advanced as UK, Germany or France. Like my aunt she was a very good student, who wanted to study math and physics. However, while her parents supported her, Bolsheviks stopped her from any education. She then quickly escaped from Poland with the help of her family to Paris, France. There she was admitted to Sorbonne University, where she met her future husband Prof. Currie. She and her husband made contributions to science, such that they were awarded the first Nobel Prize in physics ever given. After her husband's death, she took his position and continued her work and was awarded a solo Nobel Prize.

She was also a family woman and had three daughters, one of whom, Juliet won a Nobel Prize in physics. Also, her third daughter's husband, a peace activist, received a Nobel Prize for peace. There were four Nobel prizes in that family. I compare Masi with Marie Currie because we will never know if, given the chance, she could have been a Nobel laureate too. Another example, in San Francisco, USA a 98 year old woman recently graduated from high school, 80 years after she left school without a diploma. She is Josephine Belasco, who still goes out with friends , reads the newspaper and cooks Italian dinners for her family. She says she always regretted dropping out of Galileo High School in San Francisco, CA. (Los Angeles Times reporting).

I end it here saying that women can advance in life and contribute for the betterment of society only if the men advance themselves in their thinking and take the women along as equal partners and not as subservient second class citizens.

That get together in Kolkata inspired me to write about the women in my life who influenced me in various ways. My cousin Kalyan, (Kaju), my aunt's second son who was a writer and published some books, wanted to write about my life. At the time it did not work out and I left Kolkata for the USA. He would have written the book in Bengali. Since then he has passed away.

My thoughts & background

I was born in Varanasi, India in an upper middle class family. I moved to the USA more than four decades ago. I did not know the caste system that should have categorized me as to where my family belonged in the caste hierchy. I am sure it still exists in India as I write this. Certain things do not disappear, despite the laws that are passed to outlaw them. The caste system is outlawed in India. We in the USA know discrimination in every phase of life. However, we are free to discuss what ever discrimination bothers us that is not politically correct; attempts could be made to correct them by passing amendments at election time. In India, people do not fight for their rights as much as they do in the U.S. leading the way to the Fundamentalists who decide how one should live.

Recently, I read an article in the Los Angeles Times about Varanasi, India, the holy city of Hindus where I was born. In this article the writer talks about "plight of Hindu widows". The article talks about a movie called *Water* made by the Writer-Director Deepa Mehta in which she portrays widows, ages from 8 to 80, in a Varanasi Ashram. This movie was an academy award nominated foreign film from Canada. From the article I gathered Deepa Mehta had a lot of trouble filming that in location at Varanasi. Many interfered with her filming. Finally she packed off and landed in Srilanka to complete her project. In Ancient India an Ashram was a place for the saints to retire in a peaceful tranquil place in nature, but the Ashram in Varanasi is nowhere near the Ancient Indian Ashram. There are many Ashrams in Varanasi. This article brought back a lot of memories and I remembered those women clad in white sheets or saris. In my household some were even hired as cooks. Those days I was too young to think and I did not know how to determine the bad and evil in such places. It is quite an eye opener for me to see how much cruelty still exists there. I feel there is a built–in inertia in Hindu society regarding women. If she is a widow, she is a sinner, and therefore she lost her husband and deserves all the punishments that are prescribed in Manusmiriti, the Hindu holy text.

In a similar documentary film called: *Hidden away Slave girls of India,* globe-trotting television journalist, Lisa Ling portrays a dismal picture of 60 million Indian children, mostly girls as child laborers and prostitutes. In this made- for- television program, Ling tells poignant stories of young girls who were forced into child labors as domestics and prostitutes. However, there was a little hope when she showed a 19 years old ex- prostitute who is now an activist working to end such activities. In another recent PBS (Public Broadcasting Service) television program I watched with awe how in Indian state of Rajasthan children under the age of 10 are married off by the parents. While a boy-child grows up without problems, a girl- child is treated miserably by the "mother in law" in her new home such that she ends up in shame back with her family. These child-marriages are very common in Rajasthan.

This philosophical social backwardness among women is compounded by Islamic culture also. Aiyan Hershi Ali, a renowned author talks about Islamic woman as a pious slave. Her book "Infidel" describes how a Muslim woman is treated in an Islamic country. Another Muslim woman, Taslima Nasrin of Bangladesh, a physician, who speaks and writes against the world's religions, particularly Islam for denying equal rights to women, believes the Fundamentalists are responsible for fomenting hatred among people of different faiths. She fled her Islamic country, Bangladesh to escape death threats and now lives in Kolkata, India. However, even in democratic India, some Muslim clerics do not leave her alone. They are trying to compel the Indian Government to take action against her, and throw her out of India. I do hope India does not bend under the pressure of the Islamic clerics and lets her stay safely. I do hope Muslim women realize how the religion holds them back, and it is up to them to rise against the fundamentalist pressures. Recently, Microsoft, the U.S. software company saw its effect firsthand in India. In an effort to help Muslim women, who are very good at a special embroidery work called Chikan embroidery, in the northern city of Lucknow, UP, Microsoft funded $100,000.00 for Software Company Datamation to develop software to help Chikan embroidery in design and give it a modern business model. However, most of the families refused to let their unmarried daughters participate in such an opportunity. Some families banned unmarried daughters from taking full time design roles, which involves interaction with buyers, designers, etc. Sometime ago while shopping in Macy's, a big department store in USA, I noticed a woman's shirt with Chikan like embroidery displayed prominently, I was curious, because I thought Chikan had finally arrived in the Western world. When I closely examined the shirt, it was MADE IN CHINA, not in India. Despite India's computer advancement, social conservatism is depriving the country from full participation by the work force. In this modern time it is a huge economic waste for India.

Questions most often asked me by Americans are about the caste system and dowry and also about an outlawed custom known as Sati. I answer most of the time "all are outlawed in the Indian Constitution" I know the caste system is still practiced de facto, but not as much as before, and dowry is very much in existence. In some states a man starts saving money as soon as a girl child is born, not for her education but for her wedding. An American television co. CBS program "60 minutes" presented two programs; one was a wedding in New Delhi, India, in which a bride revolted against the greedy dowry- demanding groom's family, and walked out of the elaborate marriage ceremony. I commend that girl for her courage and wish Indian women, en mass would revolt against the dowry system. The other, about how Indians treat the untouchables, demonstrated how lowest class workers are given jobs clearing all the fecal material without proper sanitary precautions. I think men should go into overdrive to right such abominable ways in the society. These are the people converting their religion from lowly Hindu to Buddhist, Christian or Muslim. Recent history records that Ambedkar, a national leader in independent India who happened to be of the lowest caste, converted to Buddhism to demonstrate the plight of the Caste system; however, this gets transposed into the newly minted Christian, Muslim or Buddhist. I understand in South India there are churches for "higher caste or lower caste Christians". And in a huge catholic church, St. Mary's in Trichinapalli, Tamilnadu (previously Madras state) people sit and pray in their respective designated areas meant for different "caste-Christians". This was the custom about 45 years ago. How they pray at the present time, I do not know. Fast forward, to a recent article in the Medical Evangelist, an Adventist publication, Spring/Summer, 2007 issue. David Catalano, MD writes "the state of Andhra Pradesh is predominantly Hindu, with a Christian Governor. The majority of new converted Christians are Adventist Christians in this region. God has seen fit to open the floodgates to over 150,000 souls in our church alone over the decade, whereas just hundreds had been baptized in previous years. He says harvest is ripe, resulting in hundreds of new churches being built, averaging one for every day of the year". This accelerated speed to convert Hindus to Christianity is due mainly to the unhappiness that exists in Hindu society due to the caste system. Missionaries dare not go to a Muslim country and try to convert them to Christianity. India is a secular democracy; therefore, certain freedoms exist for the Missionaries to preach their religion. Furthermore, I hope that while Missionaries are helping to convert to Christianity, they also teach the new converts how to be responsible citizens in a democratic country like India and live in harmony with all the people of various religious pursuits.

The women there are not strong enough to bring in drastic changes in their social customs, and men are, by and large, not interested in social changes, which are not in their interest, and perhaps greed plays a big role in maintaining the dowry system. And that is why it continues.

Lastly, Sati, a heinous custom in which a young widow is burnt to death justifying her worth only in relation to her man, well illustrates woman's lack of status as individuals in ancient India. My research about this custom tells me that it is as ancient as the caste system, and was formulated by Manu in Manusmriti many centuries back. He said a woman if widowed, shall remain pure and chaste and was not to remarry, while a man was permitted to marry again. This over the years, from about 700 AD, evolved into the ritual of self-sacrifice by a widow on her husband's pyre. That way she remained true to her husband. I believe this was the way men dispensed with the women as unnecessary baggage and named it self-sacrificing Sati. This was prevalent in some states such as Rajasthan, Gujarat and Bengal, now West Bengal, and mostly in the warrior class or Khatriya of the caste system. The dead women were idolized and people paid them great respect. Tombstone like markers were put up at the sites. Under British rule this custom was banned in 1829. However, it was revived in the independent India, and the government outlawed it again in 1956. Perhaps the Indian government was not strictly observing, so there was a second resurgence and then a prevention ordinance was passed in 1987.Occasionally, even now, I read in the newspapers about an episode of such a "sacrifice." I believe the status of women should be looked at very critically.

This is as good a place as any to write my thoughts about "Cremation" itself, keeping in mind how we humans are sending our planet Earth spiraling downwards. Hindus in particular are doing a lot of damage to global-warming. It appears it is not going to change soon. The reports suggest that funeral needs strip the country of more than 50 million trees a year. To make one pyre to burn one corpse takes about 800 pounds of wood, and in an overpopulated country that is a lot of wood to keep the burning places in operation. This method also releases copius carbon dioxide, and that pollution contributes to global warming, plus the fact that the trees are being cut down, and therefore, they are not there to utilize carbon dioxide in photosynthesis to take care of the pollution. I hope the Social Scientists, Public leaders and Scientists take an active role to convince the religious Pundits to improvise the rituals like " mukhagni" and kapal kriya" and usher in "green pyres" as is provided by Anshul Garg of Delhi, Director of Mokshda and also popularize Crematoria. Furthermore, unburned body parts are dumped into the waterways which increases the toxicity of the already polluted water. It is a huge problem that needs to be solved.

While writing this, I thought to look into the status of women in the U.S. as the new world was taking shape. The women were always subservient to their male counterpart, and men told them that it was "God's will". Women however, gradually chipped away this concept of "God's will" and eventually took their rightful place in society. They energized the female population and with persistent courage and will-power demonstrated that any thing is possible to achieve. They voiced their opinions against slavery and acted as abolitionists, by writing diaries and letters. Harriet Beecher Stowe took it further by writing the book "Uncle Tom's Cabin", which she wrote in 1852, in which she was voicing against the slave owners, mostly men, who also said it was God's will to enslave certain people. While all this was going on, Black women slaves were fighting their own fights to free themselves from slavery and inhumane treatment at the hands of slave masters. The women gave their own interpretation of God's will, and Sarah Grimke, a white woman, from a slave owner family wrote "I ask no favors for my sex." Further she wrote, "All I ask of our brethren is that they will take their feet from off our necks and permit us to stand upright on the ground which God has deigned us to occupy". I am not mentioning here about the Indian (American) women who were quite free and almost matriarchal. The women put up their fights for equality and freedom, and such fighters were called Suffragists. Finally, American women were permitted to vote in the 1920 November election. This is very well documented by Donna M. Lucey in "I Dwell in Possibility, women build a nation 1600-1920." What a contrast between two women populations.

My Grandmother

I grew up mostly in my maternal grandmother's house; she lived in a huge mansion in Varanasi. My grandfather owned a lot of land (such landlords are called Zamindars). My grandma, Kamala Devi came from a very rich family in Calcutta (Kolkata). At the time, Calcutta was the capital of British India, and a lot of trade took place between the UK and India, via East India Co. at Calcutta. My grandma's father was in the export business, mostly cotton products to the UK.

He was a rich man. He loved his little girl, Kamala very much, but according to tradition at the time, she was married off at the tender age of 10 or 11 to my 18 year old grandpa from Varanasi, hundreds of miles away from Calcutta. A marriage was arranged, between two good families. This child bride, Kamala Devi would have also gone to an Ashram if my grandpa had died at an early age. Thank god, both my grandparents lived in their eighties and nineties. We grand kids were grandma's favorites, and we preferred to stay with her whenever our mothers let us. Of the eight grandkids, I was the one who stayed with her the most. Later, my sister Mira lived with her for a number of years.

My grandmother was a very pious, simple woman; she used to prepare elaborate meals for the whole family and also for a few servants. She spent all her life in the kitchen and was a very good cook. I had never seen her wear a sweater or use a wrapper to ward against cold weather, because she spent her time in the warmth of the kitchen.

She rested later in the evening, after finishing her chores, reading some Bengali magazines, *Probasi, Basumati* etc.; perhaps these are no longer in circulation.

She used to tell me stories about herself. She grew up at her in law's place as a neglected step child. Her father in law was a strict disciplinarian, and a very rough and angry man. Grandma's job was to serve his meals, and she would be very scared to go out there with the food plate to serve him. This man had opinion about every thing that went on in the household. The idea to strip off clothes and keep the bare minimum of a wrap around sari only for the young kid-bride was his, and nobody had the guts to talk him out of it. That explained why she looked very unassuming, dressed in ordinary clothes, with no wardrobe of any kind. If there was an occasion that needed her to dress up a little, my mother would go shopping for her. The way she was treated was unconscionable.

She and grandpa had separate bed rooms. Now as I look back it was hard to tell if they were a married couple. Now I think as if they were separated. I never heard them sit together and discuss the household problems of any kind. My grandma had very good health; I must say she had good genes. I never saw her sick and lying down, perhaps austere living helped. She told me all about the jewelry that her father had given her as a wedding gift. It was hard to comprehend, but I got the impression that she was almost encased in gold. In India the gold in jewelry is almost pure. But all that jewelry was stolen one night at her new place. That was the end of her life; no body replaced her jewels, or gave her any more. For an Indian woman jewelry is a sort of security net in life, so my grandma was heart broken, and no body comforted her. Her father, far away in Calcutta was not informed about his daughter's misfortune. Soon after her father committed suicide because he lost his business, thus his livelihood, but this was not disclosed to his daughter, Kamala in Varanasi either. She learnt of her father's death much later.

Her life was like a road side weed which gets trampled every now and then and still lives.

As a little girl I was determined not to have a married life like my grandma. All those days with her left a lasting impression which was not very pleasant to me about married life; this was compounded by another happening that took place a few years later, which I will write about later. I always felt sad for my grandma. But, I was also close to my grandpa. He was the one who told me all about Shakespearian literature, when story- telling at night after dinner before going to bed. He had a law degree, and was an English scholar; he never practiced law, however.

In India, the girls are taken care of by their fathers and they are married off. As a wife, they look forward to giving birth to a few boys, anticipating the later years; these boys will take care of the mother. My grandma had two boys, but they never took care of her, even though they inherited all the property. She spent her last days with her daughter Shanti Rani. My mother, Shobha Rani also took care of her after my grandpa was gone. After my grandpa's death, a Will was read in which all the landed property and cash were given to my two uncles (grandmas' two sons) but nothing much to the women, e.g. Kamala Devi, Shanti Rani and Shobha Rani. It was presumed that daughters were married off, and got their share as dowary, therefore no share in the Will. Grandma was never mentioned in the Will. I believe, grandpa decided she will be looked after by her sons. My grandfather left a lot of cash. He owned a lot of agricultural property in another state, Bihar. The main cash crop was rice. My grandpa and his brother's family recognized that the land reform was sure to come. Under that law all that property would have gone. This was happening just before independence was declared for India in 1947. Therefore, at a very opportune time, they sold all their property, and they were no longer Zamindars

After grandpa's death, his two sons took the cash and left my grandma at that mansion, without any arrangements as to how she will live there. My sister Mira who was doing her BA degree at the time, decided to stay at Grandma's and take care of her. She was physically fit and at that time she was about 60ish, but no hypertension, diabetes or high cholesterol that we knew of at the time. In comparison to my present health and suffering, taking all sorts of medicine. She was a female who exhibited no emotional variation one way or another.

After High School, I moved to Lucknow where my parents lived, to start my college education. I did my degrees at the local University. We were quite a few students in the junior college but only a few went for a science degree. We were only five or six students in a coeducational class of 150 students. We six women waited out side for the Professor to enter the class, and then we would file into the class behind him. We sat in the front row seats, and after the class we filed out with the teacher. We had to dress very modestly, not to attract any attention. After I finished my Premedical and graduate degree I took a break from studies and started a teaching job.

A few years later I returned to Varanasi again to a teaching position at the University. I decided to live at a university Housing. With me moved my grandma and my sister too. We had a good life, and slowly got used to living in a smaller house and in academic surroundings. The house we left behind was huge; it had many bed rooms, living rooms, vegetarian, non vegetarian kitchens, meditation prayer and a delivery room where we were born and so on. Once in a while I would sneak in the prayer room of my grandpa hoping to see some supernatural happening, but never noticed any. One episode that I mentioned earlier without giving details will be appropriate to write about now. I was about eight years old when my aunt (Grandma's daughter in law) came to have her first baby there. She had a normal pregnancy, my father helped her with her pregnancy up keep. A midwife was in touch, and she would help deliver the baby. My aunt went to the delivery room. Soon she was in labor pain, and was moaning and groaning so much that it became unbearable for me to listen. I was trying to go as far away as I could to avoid her moaning. I finally ended up in the third floor terrace, where it was not audible any more, and I fell asleep there. My older sister was looking for me and found me there. When we returned to the first floor, I saw the little dead baby wrapped in a white cloth taken away for its last rights. My aunt was sad but all right. That episode totally changed my mind for good about ever getting married.

To continue about the house that we left behind which had Tennis and Badminton courts and a back yard that was like a small Botanical garden. There were numerous huge shade, flowering and fruit trees. All this vegetation was well landscaped within a gated compound. From the gate there was a path way leading to the house. There were shrubberies and flowering trees on the side of the pathway, and shade trees by the boundary wall. They were: fruit trees such as Guava, Pomegranate (*Punica granatus*), and Bael tree (*Aegle marmelos*), Ficus (ficus glomerata), Banana, Grape fruit (Citrus aurantica), Lemon, Drumstick (*Moringa olifera*), Phalsa tree (*Greuria* asiatica). The shade and ornamental trees were: Debdaru, Indian mast tree (Polyalthea *longifolia*), Neem (*Azadirachta indica*) Bakul tree, India's intoxicating garland flower (*Mimusops elongi*), Shuli tree (*Nyctanthus arbortristis*), *Artocarpus*, a tropical tree and Magnolia (*Magnolia grandiflora*), beautiful kachnar (*Bauhenia*) and Oleander. Flowering plants like Roses, Gardenias were in flower beds around a huge lawn. There were creepers growing on the boundary wall, they were railway creeper and Madhabilata (*Quisquitis indica*), and others I do not remember now.

All this was hard to maintain, and needed a lot of help, which my grandma did not have. My uncles left her in a swim or sink situation. One day, as I returned from my teaching job, I found that my grandma was gone. My housekeeper told me some guy came and took her away. I knew right away who the guy was. From the description given to me I knew it was my uncle (her older son) who came from Calcutta and took his mother away only to deposit her with my aunt, which I learned later. He thought I was a threat to his property if grandma stays with me. It was one of the worst days in my life.

Indirectly, grandma shaped my life, and I was getting stronger to deal with life's problems. A few years later when I was a fellow at University of California Los Angeles (UCLA), one day I decided not to go to work, as I had an intense feeling that I would hear some bad news. As the day went on and I got my mail, there it was. My beloved grandma was gone. She had passed away quietly at her daughter's place in Calcutta.

My Mother

It appears to me as if mother has never left me, even though she left this mortal world a few years ago. I am not going to delve into dreaming, and can we relate a particular dream to what is happening at that moment, for me this was not a random electrical flash. I can still remember the episode vividly. After the millennium eve, I returned to my home in Murrieta, California on the first of the year. I had spent the Christmas holidays with friends in Ohio. I had had dinner with some other friends in their farm house, who were hog farmers. I was told that some people in the family were very sick with diarrhea, vomiting etc. Back in California my German friends invited me to have lunch in a local restaurant, but I was already feeling sick. Very soon I was violently sick, very active at both ends, and I knew I was becoming dehydrated. My friend Trudy brought me some home made soup and a drink called Gatorade which I had requested. I was becoming very weak, and trying to rest in between trips to the bathroom. It was that afternoon as I was half a sleep, that I felt my mother was sitting on the corner chair neatly dressed in her white sari. It was so real that I got up and started looking for her in every room and my doggie, Tim Tim followed me. Mean time the phone rang; my German friend was calling to enquire how I was feeling. I told her I was looking around for my mother and I would call her back. She did not say anything to me. Soon after I realized I was dreaming or hallucinating and that my Ma was not alive, I called my friend back and told her how real my mother's image was and so on. However, she had already talked with other local German ladies saying that I was loosing my mind, and she was quite concerned about it.

I slowly recovered from my Norwalk viral infection after I obtained medicine for my symptoms. However, I was quite convinced that my mother was looking over me.

I realize mothers have the most difficult task in the world, be it in the East or West, but that is where the similarity ends, because in India the social philosophy that guides the women about how to raise children is quite different. The foremost difference is that a female child is unwanted, therefore, raised without much care. At present in India, fetal technology in Medicine has contributed to this immensely, resulting in 10 million female fetuses being aborted yearly. This is at par with China, where they control the population. Indian female children are malnourished compared to male children; consequently such children do not grow to be healthy adults. But who cares?

My mother gave birth to four of us, all girls. Thank god they did not do fetal research then. She raised us without any kind of bias; I did not realize this bias existed until later. We were born at my grandma's, and she had no problem accepting us as girls. I was her favorite grandchild. I wonder how these women perpetuate destruction of their own kind, generation after generation. My aunt, mother's older sister had four boys. We grew up together without any gender bias.

Unlike my grandma, mother was well groomed; it appeared to me she was raised differently than her mother, who was an outsider. My mother dressed well, she was quite fashionable in her time. That is as far as it went. She and her sister were taken out of school soon after they were admitted, and they were schooled at home which was not much; she was married off at age 16. While she was growing up she was good in sports, and she played Badminton and Tennis with her cousins. She had a lot of interest in gardening. She loved animals; her pet was a lame deer. She told us stories about animals. One such story I remember very well was about a horse owned by the family. Her uncle, my grandpa's older brother whom she adored very much, went to work by horse driven carriage. One day when he was returning from work, his enemies tried to attack him by assaulting the coachman. However, the horse did not stop instead he speeded up and stopped only when he brought the master inside the residential compound. The coachman was hurt badly, but was not dead. That story impressed me very much about those handsome horses and how obedient and caring these animals are.

She wanted to study science and dreamed of going to Uppsala, Sweden for studies, but never went beyond the gates of their home. She read a lot and had a lot of general knowledge. I spent most of my childhood at my grandma's so I did not have much chance to learn about her growing up life.

My mother did not have a very good married life, her mother- in-law; my other grandma was not a very pleasant person. The family lived in a town far from Varanasi, it was a large family, of four girls and four boys. Four of the eight aunts and uncles in the family, who were not married, particularly women were always critically assessing my mother. Consequently, my grandmother picked on her and made her life unbearable. My father at the time was still finishing his medical school, away from that town, was not there to interfere on her behalf. I believe even if he had been there he would not have said much against his domineering mother.

My mother on her parent's advice came to live at my grandma's. My grandma was getting older, and therefore, having my mother there; semi permanently was good for the family. My mother assisted to run the day to day affairs of the family. I remember that since then we had some very sumptuous non vegetarian foods prepared by my mother, we always looked forward to her non vegetarian dishes. I did not see any recipes that she followed to cook those delicious foods, however, so we did not learn how she cooked, and I regret that. In India, cook books were almost non existent at the time. Now of course, there are a few cook books appearing in India. These books are not as well written as in the West. In the west, a cook book is like reading a biochemistry laboratory hand book, in which every thing is spelled out in detail, whereas, Indian cook books will give you every thing in approximation. This in a nut shell also tells the differences between an Indian kitchen and a western Kitchen. My kitchen in the U.S. is almost like a small Biochemistry lab. A refrigerator, oven with top burners, microwave oven, dishwasher in addition to various other gadgets, are common in the west. In India the kitchens are sparsely furnished and not much fun to work in. Above all they do not utilize the refrigerator for what it is designed. In some homes it sits in the living room as a status symbol. They do not believe in eating left over foods so the food has to be cooked fresh every time they eat. This is one job a woman has to do; some lucky ones have help every step of the way.

Once a year my aunt and her family came to visit us for Dasaherra holidays. This is a Bengali festival in which goddess Durga is worshipped, those were my memorable days. We looked forward to playing with our four cousins. My mother was in charge of our food, so at dinner time she collected all eight kids, and sat in a circle and fed us the food served on a big plate, one by one. This mode of feeding was discontinued when the older kids felt embarrassed. We had good times climbing fruit trees, such as guava and mangoes, we also collected bags full of flowers, such as yellow oleander, wild roses for a temple nearby. In the evening we would dress up in good clothes to attend the festivities. After a few happy days when my aunt and her family would leave, all of us would go to the railway station to say goodbye to my aunt and family. We hung around the departing family and waited on the platform until the train left and then we returned to our routine schedule after the train pulled away from the platform. One year, while we were milling around with the family at the railway station to send off my aunt and family, my father discovered his youngest daughter was missing. We started looking around to find her. My youngest sister was at the time about four years old. She was a little girl with light complexion. That day my mother had dressed her in a navy blue white polka dot dress. She was a very cute, attractive little girl. My father found her, held by an English military young fellow, called a Tommy. There were quite a few of those British Tommies on the platform at the time, waiting for the same train. My father finally took away his little girl. The Tommy expressed his desire to adopt the little girl and bring her to England. My father said thank you, but sorry you can not have her. After this episode, my parents kept a constant watch on us, particularly my little sister. Later in her life she became mother of a little girl herself, who was born and grew up in Germany, became a lawyer, and is now getting ready to marry an English lawyer. So there is my sister's English connection, which I shall write about later.

We loved summers, though sometimes temperature reached 120 F. My grandma would arrange wooden flat beds on the back yard lawn, with very little mattresses on them, and we slept there at night under the star studded sky, until the rainy season came.

We were getting ready to be admitted to a school and my mother was determined that her daughters be given all the education that they can take. My father supported her decision. Of course, my mother remembered her days when she and her sister were taken out of school soon after they were admitted.

We were admitted at the same school where my mother was admitted when she was a little girl, but we were taking the school bus instead of a horse driven carriage. It was a girl's school. Things had changed but very little since her childhood days.

This was the beginning days of World War II and even though India was not in the war, we felt its effect in every way including the platform encounter with a Tommy, after all we were British subjects, and Britain was very much in the war. My father and uncle were serving in the British army. By the way Tommy is not a derogatory word; this just denotes a white English guy in the infantry.

Those days my mother was left alone to raise us single handed. However, she was operating under the security of a joint family system. One day my mother was going to the store with her younger brother and soon there were rumors that in the absence of my father, my mother was having an affair, of course, such baseless rumors die soon. Those days' women did not move around outdoors unescorted. She supervised every aspect of our lives, including home work. Money was tight for her, therefore, she worked nonstop. After finishing her household chores, she sat down with her Singer sewing machine and sewed all our clothes, including our undergarments. In India ready made clothes were non existent those days; people would hire tailors and have things sewed. My mother was a very good tailor. The girls in my class always appreciated my dresses tailored by my mother. She of course did not sew men's clothes; those were done by our family tailor. During winter time she bought wool and knitted sweaters for all of us. She was a tireless worker. In her spare moments, she would even do some embroidery and work on burlap pieces to create beautiful designs, which we used as Asans or mats to sit on on the floor, and I can't appreciate enough what she did. I wish I was nice to her then. Here in the U.S., people save such handcraft creations and pass them on from mother to daughters as an inheritance. I know of a lady who catalogued all her belongings to put in her Will detailing what will go to whom. But in India there is no such thing as saving, every thing gets trashed. Furthermore, women do not write a Will.

My mother was also very conscious of her health, because she had suffered from a vitamin deficiency disease called Beriberi. She, therefore, learned the benefits of good eating and exercise. To do her exercise every day, she walked 100 times around our second floor verandah, which was about one tenth of a mile long, she took close to an hour to cover those 100 times. To keep up with her physical activity she gardened and raised vegetables. I left my family at a very early age, so my youngest sister was the one who gave my mother her support and company. She took her to movies and musical functions and traveled with her to places for vacation. But my father also was not keeping good health, therefore she became house bound, and my sister also had left after getting married. My mother lived long like her mother and sister, but her quality of life was also not very good. But I am comparing life in the U.S. and India, in my last visit when she was still alive, I felt so depressed seeing her failing life and knowing there was not much I could do. She was also suffering from dementia or Alzheimer disease, therefore did not recognize me. That affected my sister a lot more than me. One way to take care of the situation was to leave the U.S. and move back there and take care of her remaining days. But it was very frustrating for me to go through every level of burocracy to get any thing accomplished. With her Alzheimer she knew who her care-giver was, therefore, I left her with my nephew, her grandson and I kept financing until she was gone. At the end, I was praying to God to relieve her from this mortal life. This was also one of my very sad days. She passed away at age 92.

We did not lead a very exciting life. Going to school was a big thing in our lives. I used to bring English books from the school library that opened the window for me to the western world. I also read all kinds of Bengali writers like Tagore, Bonkim and Sarat Chatterji and others. I studied Hindi as my vernacular, so I read three languages simultaneously. Hindi and Bengali are two different Indian languages, not only different in dialect but they differ also alphabetically. Through these different readings I was forming different ideas about my growing up and the backwardness of women that existed in our society. Sarat Chatterjee's books had laid out very well how men dominated women because they provided shelter and food for them, but the women have inner strength to withstand all that and some. But I feel Indian women are falling behind in the world in comparison to women of other countries including China and Japan. Of course, I changed my mind about Japanese women, because quite a few of them came to live with me in the USA, which I shall write about later. In my discussions with other Indians about Indian women, they disagreed with me totally and to prove their point, would throw at me some of the marquee names such as Indira Gandhi, Sarojini Naidu and others to demonstrate that Indian women are just as good as others. Of course, I saw an Indian woman pilot flying an Indian Airlines Boeing 737 jet liner between Delhi and Jaipur. In the U.S., there are two Indian women who have gone on space flights. That is a very elite select group of people. But this is not the norm by any means, but a rarity. This however, tells us that they could achieve a less subservient life if they want to. In general, I feel they don't put forth an effort to improve their daily lives, yet they will not hesitate to buy expensive saries, gold and diamond ornaments. The ornaments are put in a vault; if left at home they may be stolen, and a silk sari will be eaten up by some pests.

Our Childhood

When we four sisters were growing up, our lives revolved around going to school and doing home work. I did not keep a diary, so I depend on my memory to talk about my life. I earned quite good grades in every subject and I had more interest in science and math. Suddenly, my grades started going down ward, and I became evasive about my life. I was suffering from angst, because I was in the beginning of puberty, and there was no help to guide me through that difficult time in my life. My mother was too busy with her daily chores, and my older sister perhaps was not observant enough. My mother noticed my anatomic change, and provided me with a bra, but she did not realize my other problem. Not knowing what was going on, I thought I had probably caught some miserable venereal disease, how, I did not know. This is the way I was for a few months, until finally, my sister told me this is part of growing up.

Later I learned that a generation ago when a girl entered puberty she would stay in one place, locked up in a room, because she was considered unclean until she was done with her periods. This way every body came to know what she was going through. That custom was discontinued at the time we were growing up. So there was no way to learn about a change in life. I hope the girls in India are better prepared now to enter puberty. After my sister briefed me about womanhood, my grades also improved, but my care free life was gone. I am not blaming my mother or my older sister; these were the inadequacies of life in India. This is the way we grew up, being evasive. Like-wise, I also did not notice when my next sister was going through my predicament. I hope, at present girls have sexual awareness. I do not dare think about how those young girls were pushed into getting married at a tender teenage and endured the first day of a married life together.

My oldest sister finished High School and prepared to go to college, it was a big achievement in our family for a female to go to college. But nothing was done to celebrate the occasion. When my turn came to take my High School examination, I realized how hard it was. Unlike in the U.S., HS exams in each state are given by a big examining administrative office. The examination centers distribute the examination papers to the students at the same time all over the state, this goes on for days. After couple of months the results are announced in the local newspapers. It is a traumatic time for the students waiting for the results. If your name is not printed, you have failed the exam. A lot of failed students take their lives when the result is announced. I learnt that Japanese students likewise commit suicide when they fail the exams. In the U.S. students have it easy.

The school system in India, however, needs to change the way students are taught. I remember that most of my learning was just memorizing everything without reasoning. We dare not question our teachers even if we wanted to, consequently the classes are non reactive, with no participation by the students. The teachers teach and move on. I hope it is changing for the better. In the U.S., High Schools are falling behind other industrialized nations, yet the science projects they compete in once a year are of excellent, high grade standard. They also excel in spelling and geography knowledge competitions. Such activities are non existent in India, so the students are bookish and noninspiring and without curiosity. In that education system no creativity was encouraged or stimulated. Another lack of activity for a student is sports, in India there is hardly any emphasis on sports. The result of this is evident every four years while the Olympic Games are played and India is no where to be seen.

I did not participate much in sports either, because it would take away my study time. It seems with the advancement of Neuroscience technology scientists are proving ancient Greece was right, that physical fitness is equally important for a sound, fit body and intelligent mind. No wonder they started the Olympics.

My Aunt

Before I write about my sisters, I should talk about my aunt. I started writing this as I mentioned in the beginning because I was asked by my cousin to introduce my aunt at her anniversary celebration. My cousin, her oldest living son, was her favorite of four sons, and it is customary for her to spend her last days with him and his wife. She loved her other sons also but at least she was very diplomatic about it. It was nice of them to celebrate her life, though I could not quite see anything spectacular to talk about. She was a very lucky woman, because she gave birth to four sons. She did not have to worry about getting a daughter married and for that to start saving for a dowry. On the other hand she was in a position to become rich with incoming dowry when the sons were to be married. My aunt like my mother was also a forward- minded person; as far as I know she never asked for dowry when her sons were married, each one was an arranged marriage though. I must say a good word for her husband. My uncle who was also not a greedy man, out to get rich with the sons weddings. We need more men like him.

She always wanted to have a daughter, so she asked my mother to let her have one of her daughters. My mother agreed, and thought I would be the best candidate, because I was capable of living without other siblings. I was ready to go but at the last minute I felt cold feet and backed out of the deal. We loved our aunt very much, and she loved us also as her own kids, but somehow I did not want to leave my own family. We looked forward to visiting her during our summer vacation and to her visits with her family during holidays. She always brought us modern fashions from Calcutta. Later I continued to visit her whenever I could. When her oldest son returned from Germany after four years stay there, he declared he was in love with a German girl and wanted to marry her. My aunt asked my mother and me to go there and help persuade her son to give up that marriage, and listen to his parents and marry a girl of their choice. Well, we traveled to Calcutta and talked with my cousin about the virtues of Indian women, and that they are no way inferior to any western or German woman. I was talking all that sense to him without thinking that he fell in love with a girl that had nothing to do with eastern or western culture. I did not know how much I helped the situation but eventually he backed away from that relationship and married a local woman. Who knows what influenced his change of mind; we just tried. I must say they made a good couple. I love this cousin- in- law very much, but under the circumstances her contribution to society was limited even though she is an educated woman. Not every body has to contribute; she made a good home for my cousin. I never learnt to call her Boudi or Bhabi, because she was so much younger than I.

On one of my visits I could not say good bye to one of my cousin's wives, because she was mourning her adult niece's sudden car accident death. This was because of a careless driver who did not stop while she was crossing the road. The episode reminded me of MADD (Mothers against drunk drivers) law passed in California, in which mothers who lost their kids in such car accidents, got together and lobbied to pass a law for stiff sentencing for such drivers. I felt that Indian women lack this coordinated effort and strength of mind to make things better after an adverse situation. As a matter of fact this coordinated effort is lacking in Indian society. When Mrs. Betty Ford, wife of President Ford had breast cancer, she decided to go on television and tell the whole world that she had the disease and that it is treatable and curable if it is diagnosed and caught early. In India, I knew two ladies in Varanasi who had breast cancer. Each disappeared for a long time eventually returning after having treatment in far away places, but never uttered a word about cancer. Every thing was evasive. Both the ladies were highly educated, one a Philosophy Professor and the other a Women's college Principal. They should have told the students about the dreadful disease. They were in a position to do so, but they never did and there were rumors floating around about their disease. Why they did not want to talk about it I do not know; perhaps it is a stigma they wanted to avoid as some people think it is a punishment. In a recent article in Time magazine, (Oct.15.07) Vijaya Mukherjee, a cancer survivor in Kolkata says that she is fearful to feed her own children with her own hand, thinking that the disease is contagious and pass-on to them. According to this magazine in Pune, India there is only one facility to care for 3.5 million women. Report also says half of all women with the disease go without treatment. It appears to me that in India there is a dire need for information and awareness about this disease.

In the U.S. diseases are tackled head on. For instance when the American President Roosevelt came down with Polio, people went to work to collect funds to support Polio virus vaccine research, and they started a charity. They put tin cans in every store to collect money, even a Dime; therefore it was called March of Dimes. And that is how polio virus vaccine research was financed. Now polio is almost eradicated. I do hear once in a while a sporadic polio case in India and elsewhere. I believe such national effort is unthinkable in India.

My aunt lived a long life, but her quality of life was not good. She became frail and lost most of her mobility. Indian homes are not senior-citizen friendly, therefore she struggled to move from her bedroom to her bathroom. In addition, she suffered from gynecological problem. I do not think Indian women regularly visit a Gynecologist for a cervical examination with a Pap smear. Some of these health and social problems are not talked about; I think there is a need for an Oprah Winfrey in India. This lady is an African American and a television talk show host. When she speaks people listen. I had seen Indian film star Aishwaria Rae interviewed by Oprah on one of her shows, and I was wondering why "doesn't she", A. Rae start a show like Oprah's and tell Indians how to improve their lives. People will listen to A.Rae. There is an actor, Amitabh Bachhan, who is regarded very highly by Indians and he also would go on television and talk to people about various ways to improve their lives. These actors are very powerful and they have the ability to influence change but I think they lack the vision. Another person I think of in the U.S. is Bill Clinton. This ex President, whose shine was tarnished because of the Lewinsky affair, did not retire quietly. Now a days he is busy doing good for the world. South African President Mbeki did not accept AIDS virus as the causal agent for the disease until Mr. Clinton visited him and educated him about the disease. He is now helping his own people to fight the obesity problem. Al Gore, Ex Vice President is now busy trying to bring the global warming problem to the fore front. Though I understand U.S. is still the leading polluter country in the world with China and India coming along fast. In India cities are so polluted that most of the people are suffering from respiratory problems. Indian scientists should link up with technology- oriented companies to bring their scientific knowledge to make the lives better, and to help the industries flourish without polluting. However, Industries keep polluting, and the scientists continue their research, but there is no interaction, and pollution goes on.

In India there are women Doctors, and they are trained like the men, but when they are admitted to medical college they compete for a seat with women only. There are a certain number of seats reserved for women. This was done during the British time, when a need for women doctors was recognized. Women refused to go to a man doctor perhaps they do not go to a female Doctor either. But this is one reason why there are more women doctors in India than in the U.S. I found that out when I needed some medical help when I started my life in the U.S. To my surprise I could not find a single female gynecologist in the Los Angeles area where I lived. Some of my friends referred me to a male gynecologist, and I settled for that. Things are changed now in the U.S., and one can find female doctors in any medical discipline. However, in certain fields such as Surgery, women are not represented well. I do not believe my aunt went to a gynecologist for her problems. In India women Doctors should participate in a big way to bring in disease awareness and help routine health maintenance in addition to their clinical practice. That is the only way that women's health can be improved.

My Sisters

My oldest sister, was the first one to earn a college degree in my family, and then obtained a teacher's training certificate. She was a very gentle, sweet girl, rather quiet. When my mother was pregnant with her, my grandmother had a premonition that it will be a little girl, and she had dreamed of a little girl dancing around her. She named her Gauri, after a goddess. We were not raised strictly by religion. However, we did go to temples and worshipped Gods and Goddesses. My sister used to help my grandmother to help stop days of nonstop rains by saying a prayer and lighting a candle. Most of the time it worked. We prayed a lot to Saraswati, goddess of learning. We were also taught to pray to God Shiva so that we would get a good husband. I guess I never prayed well to Shiva so no husband for me. My sister studied Philosophy and Economics, and she did very well, but as it goes in India, all she could do was to become a teacher.

She fell in love with a fellow student when she was taking her teacher's training courses, and my father was furious. We were going through very restless days. This man was of a different religion. My sister gave up her pursuit of her love life, and quietly settled down to a married life arranged by my father. This marriage was not a very happy one, but my sister was such a good person that I never heard her complain. This person was not as educated as my sister; therefore he had no respect for an educated woman. Before her marriage she was a school teacher, but he stopped her from working after they married. I never liked the guy. They had two boys and the boys are doing all right. My older nephew had an arranged marriage to a science graduate who does not utilize her education in any way. My younger nephew married his own choice. This girl is very beautiful but useless, incapable of doing anything. She is a beautician by training, but does not earn a penny. These two people have a daughter, and I understand she is very good in studies and is preparing for the entering Pre Med. Exam. I hope she makes it to Medical school. My oldest sister did not live a long life. I heard about her passing just before I was leaving on a trip to the then Soviet Union. I was very sad and the trip was very therapeutic for me. I miss her very much; she was one genuinely good soul.

My second sister, Mira was two years younger than me. She was a petite, pretty female. Like me, she also spent some time alone with our grandmother while she was finishing college. She was excellent in her studies especially in art. I have some of her paintings hanging at my place. She earned two Masters Degrees one in English and the other in Ancient history. She also was a trained Librarian, and she worked as a Librarian in a degree college. Her marriage was an arranged one too. The day my sister was getting married, of all people I felt a bit lost wondering if I was moving on the right path. There were not too many roll models for a single woman trying to live a normal life. But I quickly got over my feelings and enjoyed my sister's wedding. Even though my father did not pay any dowry, he had to spend a lot of money to take care of the wedding expenses, which consisted of a reception, dinner for a lot of people, gold jewelry and innumerable other details. I helped with the wedding sari for the bride. Her husband was a college professor, a zoologist by training and he was promoted to a Principal's position. He was frequently transferred to different government colleges and stayed away from home leaving most of his house hold duties to my sister.

I do not think there was any honeymoon period after the marriage. She raised two boys single handed in addition to keeping her full time job. She also supervised construction of their house. Once, while on site she fell and was hurt badly. Whenever I visited her I felt she was doing too much and he did not extend a helping hand to her, his alibi being I am not here, but she never complained. They had two boys, the first was born normal, and grew up to be all right. Her second pregnancy was uneventful, however, at the delivery time things did not go right, and the baby was asphyxiated. This resulted in a brain damaged baby; He grew up to be a normal man physically but with a seven year- old boy's brain. I blame her husband for not paying attention to his family. Her husband never followed a healthy life style and he suffered from all kinds of health problems, but did not visit a doctor; he died when he was in his early sixties. After he passed away, my sister almost gave up living. When I visited her in her last days, I found her to be very depressed; there was nothing for her to live for. During one of my visits at her son's house at dinner, I noticed she was not eating a meat dish and I realized she had stopped eating non vegetarian food since she was widowed. I just could not restrain myself and said, "You know today if your husband was here instead of you, he would be eating the meat dish". She just gave me a very sad look that broke my heart. My dear sister suffered from heart disease and had appropriate treatment for that, but soon stopped taking her medication. Perhaps she was looking for her exit; I felt as if a little *Sati* syndrome was working in her.

When I was in the U.S., thousands of miles away, I received the information via telepathy that she died before I received a telephone message from her son. Her passing hurt me a lot, and I cried for days.

My youngest sister, KumKum who was almost kidnapped by an English Tommy when she was a little girl, grew up at my parents, who lived away from my Grandmother. She was quite a smart and a very pretty looking girl. She was a good singer too. I remember when she was taking her B.Sc degree Examination, one day she was attacked by a predator. That disturbed her so much that she wanted to drop out of the program. My parents helped her work out of that unpleasant situation. Such men are always roaming the city streets, and help is not easily available. No body files reports with the police, because it would be considered that a woman had encouraged the man leading up to the situation. These perverted people go wild if they see Bikini- clad women of the west. Indian women do not wear a Burkha as they do in Islamic countries. Muslim women save themselves from such evil eyes hidden under the Burkha. In the West some women wear as little as possible, but men have to keep their gawking eyes to themselves. There are assaults on women in the U.S., but women dress as they please and law enforcement ensures that situation stays orderly. Sexual assault is very common in the U.S. on children and women, including elderly women living alone, but help is available, whereas in India there is no such help.

In India, there were not many professional choices available to women, nor did they have the creative vision, so women tried to become a teacher or a doctor and not much else. I helped my sister with the expenses to do her Master's degree in science and she stayed with me. During that time I went away for some military training of sorts to join the National Cadet Corps, in short NCC. When I returned, I found that my sister and a post doctoral student in the same department had become friends. Apparently, my father learnt about it and he was irate. The reason was this person came from a southern state. I heard this fellow's father was also very much against his son marrying a girl not of his choice, and from a different state, and he was ready to disown him. All these underpinnings diffused the situation, and my sister finished her studies and moved on.

She did not want to be in the teaching profession, so she chose to work in the Botanical garden, and had a good care- free life. She eventually met a man that my parents liked and she married him. This person lived in Germany and was an Engineer. Like me, she also wanted to go abroad, so she moved to Germany after her marriage. There she adjusted quickly to the German life style, and she joined the University of Cologne to do her Ph.D. It was a remarkable effort on her part, and she finished her degree successfully. Her dissertation was written in German and published. She sent me a copy. She was offered and accepted a teaching position in Germany at a government run college, which she served until her retirement. While she was doing her Ph.D degree her only daughter, Gita was born. It was a struggle for her to raise her daughter and keep her job and take care of the household chores but she was a good mother and the girl grew up and did very well academically. She was a very cute little girl. She did her Law degree in Germany at the University of Bonn, and her Master's degree in Law in London. Now she works for an American Law firm in London. Next year she is planning to marry her long time English boy friend. I have visited them several times in Germany and watched the little girl grow up.

Once my niece complained to me that I did not help my sister to come to the USA to study. I told her that I am glad I did not; otherwise we would not have you. The real reason was that when my sister wanted to come to the USA, the Viet Nam war was in full swing, and educational grants were drastically cut by the Federal Govt. As a guarantor, I had to show the immigration department that I could support her financially. Because of the decline of funds, my post doctoral fellowship was reduced to half, which was just $500.00 a month; not enough to support a graduate student. It was hard to explain all that to my niece.

Today, my sister lives a jet setter life; she and her husband have homes in Germany, India and the UK which she has decorated very well. She loves gardening and does a lot in her German home. She is a good shopper and she can spend hours shopping. She has an eye for good things including properties and without her incentive her husband would have blown the opportunity to buy their homes in Germany and London. Her husband has a wait and see attitude, that lets the deal slip away if you do not step in and act. He is a good husband and father and, being very sociable, he can start a conversation with any body, any where. Once the family was traveling and at the airport my sister and her daughter had already boarded the plane but there was no sign of him. The flight left without him and she later learnt that he missed the flight because he was engaged in a serious discussion with some one he did not even know. He then took the later flight and joined the family. Together they are doing well.

She has a whole circle of friends in Germany and India. I would like to write about her German Pen-pal here. When my sister was a little schoolgirl, my cousin who was in Germany at the time, introduced her to a little German girl of the same age. They corresponded for many years and got to know each other well through those letters. Then letter writing almost stopped as they got busy with their adult lives. In my latest visit to Calcutta, I came to know that her Pen-pal has appeared again. She had been looking for my sister's where -abouts and asked any Indian that she came across. Then she ran into this man who knew my cousin, and he came to visit my cousin in Calcutta to tell him about the Pen-pal. My cousin related that to my sister. After many years the Pen –pals got together in person in Calcutta. She came to Calcutta and stayed with my sister. She also did well in her life and is the Director of the Goethe Institute in Verona, Italy. They are very good friends, and she loves to visit India. In a way she has fallen in love with India. My sister also visited her in Verona, Italy.

As I have slowed down my sister has picked up the pace, keeping the relationship with my other sisters' families. She also keeps an eye on me, if she does not hear from me for a few days, she will call, and if she can not find me, she will call a lot of my friends in southern California. She is quite modern in thinking, and keeps track of her family's health well. When my mother passed away, she went to India and arranged the last rights for my mother and for that I am very thankful.

My Adult Life

My mother helped me significantly as I was getting on with my life after finishing my formal education. She had made many suggestions about how to set up a household for a single person. After I finished my degree I took a teaching job in a small town in a two year Junior college as it was a women's college, all my students were female. Now a days as I see all the sex related problems between the teachers and students in the U.S., I think it was not bad to have sex segregated educational institutions. Male and female students study together at degree level classes. Life was quite boring at this little town so I got together with other single teachers and started a common kitchen to prepare our meals.

Sadly, I witnessed a tragedy; a student of mine who lived in the next room where I was living committed suicide. I heard her moaning from my room, and when I went to her door it was locked from inside. Not knowing how to help her I ran around to the College authorities. Finally, when the police came and tore the door down, they found the girl comatose. They removed her, and I did not know the reason behind that tragedy. I am sure a postmortem was done, but we were not informed of any result.

Within a short time my father informed me about an Assistant Professor's level job at the university in Varanasi, my birth place, where my grandmother still lived in that big mansion described earlier. I applied and in due course, in a few weeks I was called for an interview.

I was in a big predicament because the interview date coincided with the Practical examination date for my students. The examiner was an outside man unknown to us; therefore I could leave only if I could arrange a substitute stand in for me. A colleague of mine who could stand in for me was out of town but I found her in her home town. Thank god, she agreed to return to the college and conduct the practical examination, and I took my Varanasi- bound train. If that lady had had some other engagements she would have refused me, and I would have had no interview at the University. This way I had been lucky and I moved on. My parents were very helpful. Meanwhile, my father kept sending me correspondences about prospective grooms, but I never said yes to him and slowly he learnt not to waste his time on my behalf.

At the interview, I had to face a panel of experts including the Vice chancellor of the university. I was quite nervous to face such an elite group of people, but I found a familiar face amongst them, the Head of the Department where I did my Master's. At that time I was only 20 years old. One of the experts joked about my age and remarked you must have started reading soon after you were born, and do you realize your students will be almost your age ? Even though I was very nervous I knew my Head of the Department would vote for me, and sure enough, I got the job. It was a big break in my life to jump from a junior college to a big university and I thank my father for this. When I was growing up I was not very close to my father, I used to blame him for some of my mother's problems, but I outgrew my feelings, and started appreciating his help in my life.

I started teaching at this college at the university, and I was not unduly surprised when in my first appearance to teach, the students did not stand up. It was customary then for the students to stand to show respect to the teacher, but I looked like one of them, so they did not get up. They were quite surprised to see a very young professor, which amused me.

I was getting used to the new job and living with my grandma and sister, Mira who was at the same university studying library science.

My mother wanted to sell her Varanasi rental property; therefore, she came to negotiate with the buyer. But the renters refused to vacate. Renters, in India always behave as if they will take over the property in due course, and that is what it was shaping up to be. I therefore suggested to my parents that they take the renter to court. How the court system works is very well put in the book "In spite of the Gods The strange rise of Modern India" by Edward Luce. The courts in India are slow- moving and according to him the largest backlog of cases clogging the pipeline are property- related cases. This was true decades ago, and my father traveled 500 miles round trip several times to find out that the hearing of his case was delayed. I became quite tired of this routine and decided to talk to a colleague of mine, a Politics Professor. Her husband was a magistrate, and knew the court system well including the judges. With his help my father's case was decided and the renter was finally evicted, and the property was sold. But this would not have happened if I did not have the right connections. In India nothing moves without some help. The whole experience was so frustrating, time consuming and expensive. Then there were the middlemen who were looking for money to help move your case every step of the way. I think that system has not changed much even half a century later.

The buyer of the property paid my parents cash and a few gold coins. They were not ordinary coins but they were Mogul Emperor Akbar gold coins called Mohurs. I feel rather stupid now because I converted those priceless coins into Rupees at the going gold rate instead of saving them and giving my mother money in return.

As I wrote earlier, we had moved to the university living- facility, and the worst day of my life was when my grandma was taken away by her oldest son, which left me very depressed... I always tried to see if there was any thing good to come out after hitting bottom, because at that time I felt I was free to live my life for myself. Some of my colleagues were my good friends and that helped the situation. Kamala was a lady from Madras, who taught Zoology and who was a good athlete. We got along very well, and together we went to English movies. She also invited me for some vegetarian south- Indian dinners. My other friend, Radha, was Economics Professor, and was like a big sister to me. I spent a lot of time at her place.

I started my PhD work in addition to my teaching duties. It did not create an additional financial burden, but it was quite tiring, even though I was about 24 years old. Teaching at a junior college level was not fun, because these were women not really interested in studies. They were just marking time prior to being married. These were pre medical students who probably would have competed for admission in some medical college. Most of them were mediocre in studies, but their parents would like them to be doctors. Some of them could study nursing, but that is not appreciated in the Indian society, of mostly Hindus and Muslims, whereas Christianity teaches self sacrificing services, such as Nursing. Amongst Hindus and Muslims, "a good woman" should not touch a man other than her husband, and that discourages them from becoming a nurse. This is why the predominance of Christian nurses is evident all over India. This one step below the service oriented medical profession is looked down on in India. It is a shame. I noticed this disparity when I was traveling the first time to the U.S. on a flight from New York JFK to Columbus, Ohio. My travel companions were two kids, a girl and a boy. I asked the girl where she was going. She said she is going to attend a Nursing school, and she wanted to be a Nurse. I forgot what the boy said. This was the first time I noticed the difference in the thinking of these two cultures. But I should add here that at that time girls in the USA did not have the opportunity to attend a medical school or they were discouraged to pursue medical education. Now women are studying medicine in big numbers. In India women nurses are still in short supply among Hindus and Muslims, but Indian Christian nurses, like the Indian Doctors are going all over the world.

My research was going slowly, but no body bothered me, because I had legitimate alibis. Between teaching, faculty meetings and conducting examinations, I had very little time to even go to the department. In the mean time, being the youngest faculty member, I was pushed into training in the National cadet corps. (NCC). After four months of intensive training in the infantry in Kamthi, Madhya Pradesh, I was commissioned as a second lieutenant. This was an additional part time job for me.

I did not know what to think of it at the time, but I was a good marksman, and handled both rifle and pistol well. In addition, I could send messages by Morse code, and many other things a military job demands. Overall it gave me a lot of self confidence and self reliance and a little more daring. I felt my boldness when we were camping near Lucknow, where my family lived. At the time that town was very badly flooded, and my parents were almost at the brink of being flooded. I wanted to have a closer look at the situation myself, so as an officer I got into a military truck driven by a very good driver who knew the area well. We went very close to my parent's home, but the road was closed due to the rising water and the only way reachable was by the railroad tracks. Since the trains were not moving due to the floods, the driver and I walked on the railroad tracks that lead us to the neighborhood. I carried with me some produce for the family. My family could not believe that I was the one standing at their door, and they were overjoyed to see me. I don't think I would have done this without my military training.

My military officer in Varanasi was a Major, a Kashmiri Brahmin and he was a very good man about whom I will write at a later time. This extra job was also taking my time, and I was getting further and further away from the research that I was planning to do.

My Trips to Other States

As a 2ⁿᵈ Lt, NCC officer I had to attend camps with my student cadets in far away places such as Srinagar in Kashmir, Darjeeling in West Bengal, and Shillong in Assam. I liked those trips. I traveled first class, while my cadets traveled with the rest of the population, but they did not mind. While in Kashmir, we watched India's movie stars Raj Kapoor and Vyjanthimala shooting a movie there. Raj visited us at the camp, and my cadets were happy to entertain him with a song and dance number that they had prepared for the camp closing night celebration. I also was invited because of my NCC connection, to lunches and dinners with VIPs visiting Varanasi. Most memorable were lunch with India's first Priminister Pundit Jawaharlal Nehru, and receptions for the Shah of Iran and his wife, then Soraya and Emperor Hileselasi of Ethiopia.

On my way to a camp in Shillong, then Assam, two days journey by train, I met a military officer in my compartment who was also traveling that way. This man became quite friendly with me. He probably was a Punjabi. Those days we noticed who is who state wise. This person impressed me quite a bit because of his easy going friendliness, which I thought was lacking in Indian men, and his good looks. He did leave a very good impression on me, but that was as far as it went.

At the camp in Shillong, I met a military doctor, a captain. I imagined he was a single, Bengali man, and I felt he was paying more attention to me than I needed. I was not impressed by his personality, besides; I never thought of any one in terms of selecting a life partner, in short I was not interested. A few months later, this captain showed up at my university residence in Varanasi with his mother, why I did not know.

I became quite good at organizing such trips, and I arranged a non military, exploratory trip to south India. I selected about 25 students ranging in age between 18 and 20. I also took another colleague of mine to help me on this trip, which was financed by the Indian government under some special project. We traveled by train thousands of miles to Madras, now called Chennai. Where we visited various temples. One episode I remember very well, even today and this was at Menakshi temple. Several of my girls wore Salwar, Kamiz, and one Parsee girl was in skirt and top. She was of quite fair skin. All those girls were chased out of the temple. The temple authorities were quite discriminatory, and determined that if you are not in a sari outfit, you are not a Hindu and not entitled to enter. I did not know what to think at the time.

In north India many Hindu temples were destroyed by Muslims during Mughal rule, even in the holy city of Varanasi. There, Muslims now out number Hindus and there is a mosque near every temple site. However, this Muslim culture has changed the Hindu way of thinking, and no body chases out any one visiting a temple.

From Madras we went to Trivandrum, Kerala, the southern most state of India, and the southern most tip, Cape Coumarine. There we saw the three waters from the Bay of Bengal, the Arabian Sea and the Indian Ocean meeting, and the Vivekananda Memorial. Swami Vivekananda was a saintly figure who had impressed many people in the world with his religious philosophical lectures. Modern day India lacks such figures. Greed is the name of the game now, and every body tries to make some extra money in their day to day jobs. Therefore,

India moves sluggishly even though there is much talk here in the U.S. about outsourced jobs to India.

I know corruption is prevalent in the U.S as we have seen in the Enron debacle, and also others like Tyco. They were the corrupt CEOs, but the people who do the basic jobs are rarely corrupt, so we do not have problems to get jobs done quickly. In India in order to have ordinary jobs done such as to obtain a birth or a death certificate, or a passport, one has to pay under- the-table. This goes on as an acceptable way of doing things. Years ago, I was visiting India and in those days reentry to the U.S. was difficult unless one has a vaccination certificate. I had my vaccination done in Los Angeles, USA, prior to my departure, but I forgot to pick up my certificate. When I was leaving India, I decided to vaccinate again to get a certificate from the Public health office in Lucknow, India. I did get my vaccination, but never got the certificate even though I had paid the fee for the job. The clerk in charge of issuing the certificate had alibis every time I went there; eventually I left India without the certificate. Upon arrival at LA International I told the Custom's authorities that I did get the vaccination at my Doctor's office in LA, they called the office and found affirmative and let me go. This kind of harassment is very common in India, and I feel sorry for the publicwho bear such inconveniences every day at government offices. The crooks are plentiful in the U.S. also, but they are localized, for instance Katrina relief fund. Of seven billion dollars donated by public, one billion dollars went to crooks, who just stole the money from the relief funds. And the same unaccountability of the Iraq rebuilding funds exists. Nobody knows how the billions disappeared in Iraq from the U.S. holdings.

The state of Kerala looked good to me in comparison to my northern state Utter Pradesh. Even then, almost sixty years ago Keralities were 90 percent literate, and people were less corrupt. I must say the majority

49

of people were Christians, if this has any thing to do with it, but I could not tell. From Kerala we moved to Bangalore and Mysore, in Karnataka state. At the station as we were boarding the train, I almost fell under the train as it started moving; I was saved by my students. This was like my first of nine lives. Bangalore at the time was not a vibrant town as it is today. It is now the Silicon Valley of India, and people are living relatively affluently. The neighboring princely city of Mysore was a pretty looking place with Mysore Maharaja's palace and its beautiful gardens as the main attractions. After I traveled abroad and went to visit many palaces in Europe, I felt Mysore palace was comparable to a very rich man's place, not a ruler of a state. We left the south, and traveled back home. I must say in about three weeks we saw quite a bit of India, and above all my students and my colleague returned without any health problem. Also, we found that the South was relatively less corrupt. The government offices worked without bribery. This kind of low level bribery is rampant in north India, which is unthinkable in the U.S., such petty bribery is not the modality in the U.S. government offices.

Study Abroad

Life was going on with my teaching and NCC duties, but I still wanted to do some research work and obtain a PhD degree. Therefore, I started to do some library work about graduate work in the U.S. universities. I was always fascinated by all the published work in the scientific journals and in addition, my text books for bachelor and master degrees were written by American professors. I decided on going to America even though most of my men colleagues at the department got their degrees from the UK. I was the first to go to the USA from that department. I was also impressed with the newly elected President by his personality and eloquence. He was John F. Kennedy. Those days India and USA were not politically close and USSR (Russia now) was the friendlier of the two then Super powers. However, the U.S. Embassy was trying to promote goodwill by putting up many documentaries about the contemporary America including the education system. I had attended some of those functions and I must say they had made a lot of good impressions on me.

It was not very difficult to communicate with the Chairmen or the Heads of the Departments as they are called in India, and they were prompt to reply, negative or positive. This promptness is lacking in Indian people, they do not believe in answering a letter unless it is of some interest to them. I selected about ten universities Those days I did not have a typewriter, therefore my correspondence was hand written, and I took the letters to the Post office, and made sure the stamps were defaced, otherwise the rumor was the mail collectors removed the stamps and discarded the letters, if it was mailed in a letter box. I then waited for the answers and I wrote in all my letters that I would like financial support in case I got the admission.

My mother realized that I was planning to leave India; therefore she decided that I should have some religious instruction before I left. She took me to her religion guru, who was a saintly figure in saffron robe, and he decided to give me a Mantra. This is not a baptismal ritual, but to meditate in a proper manner. He made a Puja (a prayer of sorts) infront of a small fire, and he said a few slokas (verses) in Sanskrit, then he whispered in my ear eight words, strung together as my mantra. He also gave me the mantra written on a piece of paper made into a little packet and told me to destroy it when I knew it by heart. He also advised me to meditate and repeat the mantra while meditating.

I received answers to some of my letters shortly; one could determine the letter content by weight. The slim letters informed me that financial (fellowship and such) help was not available to a beginner; in other words you have to demonstrate that your grades are good and then you can be recommended for financial assistance. But the heavy letters contained Applications and letters of recommendation forms that led me to the next step in the admission process. After this I narrowed it down to four universities. These were the ones willing to consider financial assistance.

One evening, when I returned from work I found an air letter without an envelope from an African country, Rhodesia. I wondered for a little while, as to who could be writing me a letter from such a country in Africa. To my surprise it was from one of those universities I was corresponding with. My letter was forwarded to this Head of the department, who was on his sabbatical at Rhodesia to help them develop their graduate program. He wrote that he would like to talk to me on his return trip, when he will be stopping in New Delhi to visit his ex- student who earned his degree under him. He gave me some details about his itinerary and hotel while in Delhi. I was quite thrilled because I would come face to face with a U.S. professor, as I learned later the Indian gentleman in New Delhi was the first graduate student to graduate with a PhD degree under him. My excitement died down when I realized I did not have any friend or relative in Delhi where I could stay. Staying in the Imperial hotel was out of the question. It was very expensive for an Indian Assistant Professor, so I thought I will write him a letter to say that I can not visit Delhi at the time for some reason. I procrastinated, because there was still time to write an answer as I was thinking about it.

Within a few days I got another pleasant surprise. This was a second such letter from Rhodesia, this time telling me that he will be in Lucknow to meet one of his ex students, who was the Director of an American run Literacy house in Lucknow. Therefore, I could see him there instead of New Delhi. This time I was overjoyed, because not only was it doable, but I could visit my parents who lived in Lucknow. I replied that I will be very happy to see him in Lucknow. This, as an Indian I thought was an auspicious muhurtum (moment) which came my way because of good luck. But my science background was telling me these were just coincidences that got aligned such that it worked out for me. Whatever it was, I was ready to meet the U.S Professor as I had never met an American up close and personal. I had seen American movie stars such as Charleston Hesston, Gregory Peck and others but they were stars and not regular people. Now I was going to meet a regular American.

It was a cool November morning in Lucknow when I set out for the interview. I took a cycle rickshaw to travel about 10 miles out of town in a rural area. Now I can not even imagine how I went that far by a rickshaw. This institution was started by an American philanthropist

Mrs. Wealthy Fischer who had set up a school for illiterate people. I was quite impressed by the place and the Director gave me a short tour of the facility prior to meeting the Professor. I wondered how this escaped my knowledge, and I did not know such an institution was in place in the vicinity of Lucknow, my home town.

I did a lot of home work about his research interest from the published literature, before this meeting, which was not very difficult to do. The Professor walked in with the Director, his ex student and took a seat after he shook my hand. The director left soon after. The Professor was a big man, by Indian standards. He was very well dressed, and I remember his maroon tie which looked very good on a white shirt. I remember his gold dental work which was visible when he smiled. Later, in the U.S. I learnt that gold dental work was quite common. We had a very cordial conversation and I did not have to demonstrate my research interest, only my goal and background etc that he asked about. This interview of course was not to imply that I would obtain admission to the graduate school, but that there might be a possibility for me to gain admission. He asked me if I had received an Application form, I said yes. He said he was on his way back after stops at Bangkok, Tokyo and Honolulu. He also said he will look into what the Graduate admission committee decides. Shortly before I left, he took a picture of mine. I saw that picture projected at my first departmental seminar when I joined the department. I felt very good about the meeting and I had good vibes. He knew how to make people comfortable. I returned to my work and the days and months went by without any news. I received admissions from a few places but without financial support. Another place gave me conditional support after I complete the first semester. I kept that letter in my active file.

It was summer time already and I was trying to keep up with the academic calendar. I wanted to stay in touch with research, so

I obtained a University Grants Commission summer fellowship. I selected Calcutta Bose Institute to do a short project for the summer. I selected Calcutta because I could stay at my aunt's while doing my summer research and it was economical. I had quite a good time at the institute, and learnt a lot about the techniques which I later used in my research work abroad.

One day when I returned from my research, I found a letter for me, which was forwarded from Varanasi. I had instructed the Post office to forward my mail. This letter was from the Professor, and he was giving me some good news. He said that my Application had been accepted for consideration for a teaching assistantship, which may be rejected, however, he had some research fellowships pending for which I could qualify. It was a very hot and humid day, but suddenly I felt cool. I went ahead and resigned from the Institute and prepared to apply for a Passport and a Visa at the American Consulate in Calcutta. I wrote a thank you letter to the Professor, and waited for information from the graduate School Admissions office.

I returned to my University and started preparing. The first order of business was a Passport, which took more time than it should. I filed my application and found there was a delay because I did not have enough cash for my financial back up. Those days the Government wanted cash not landed property. My father was cash poor, so he could not support my application. I was a bit sad and it was visible on my expression when I went to visit my NCC commander to tender my resignation. He straight away asked me if I was alright. He was a friendly Major, and he listened to my predicament about the Passport Application. He said no problem; I will be your financial guarantor and I got my Passport soon after that. Things were moving at an accelerated speed and I got my admission letter and I-20 to obtain my visa. But I could have my visa only after I showed the U.S. embassy that I had expenses for tuition and living etc for one quarter which was about $700.00 at the time, and the Indian Rupee was not as cheap as it is today. It was about four Rupees to a dollar. I decided to obtain a loan from Utter Pradesh Government for my expenses abroad. It was a very good loan at a very low interest rate; I was supposed to return the money after I returned from my study abroad. The other matter to take care of was to apply for leave to study abroad for about three years, which could be extended to four years. The loan application was approved and I then went to Calcutta to apply for my U.S visa at the U.S consulate. All they wanted were my Admission letter, I-20, financial assistance. I had also received a Research assistantship from the same University. The visa also required some health papers: a chest x-ray, and other health related certificates. Nowadays, I find all sorts of people are coming in without minimum health clearance, with the result that there is an increase of Tuberculosis, venereal diseases and a rare Chagas disease etc. U.S immigration is now not as strict.

My mother and aunt wanted to come to see me close my establishment so I packed my things, gave away some items to friends and left for Lucknow to prepare to leave India. While in Lucknow I took a trip to Kanpur, an industrial city where the UP government financial office was. I went there to pick up my loan money, which amounted to a few thousand rupees in cash. I took all that cash in a cloth bag, to look casual and returned to Lucknow. To my surprise, every thing went well and bureaucratic obstructions did not come into play. When I went to Calcutta to collect my visa, I had already purchased my U.S ticket at Hari Singh travel agency, a big office at the time for foreign travel. My maternal uncle helped me to buy my ticket. According to my latest correspondence with the Professor, I scheduled my arrival at a time when he would be in town so he would meet my flight. Of course, the International student's office was also in contact with me, and they too knew my arrival schedule, but they never wrote me say that they will meet my flight.

Up until then it did not occur to me how great a change that was taking place in my life. Here a little female grew up in a conservative family where girls did not do much; let alone go to America to study. For a change I felt very nervous, but I kept my feelings to my self as there was no role model to look up to, but time helps one to adjust. My family came to see me off at Delhi Palam International Airport and I was sad to leave them, but looking forward to the adventure ahead for me. My father was not so excited because he was worrying about his unmarried daughter leaving town by herself, but he lived with it.

My first stop was in Bombay, on an Indian Airlines flight. It was quite a euphoric experience seeing the plane breaking through the clouds. Soon we landed at Bombay's Santa Cruz Airport and I went straight to the hotel. Hari Singh, travel agents of Calcutta had done a good job in arranging all the hotel reservations for me. I had a good lay over in Bombay where a friend of mine came and visited me. She happened to be a NCC officer from one of the colleges in Bombay. After spending a couple of days in Bombay, I left for Geneva, Switzerland. There the hotel was on Lake Geneve, and the sight was out of this world. I had not seen such a beautiful place before. In the hotel I had a hard time handling hot and cold water taps and other contraptions, I never knew such things existed. The hotel did not have a restaurant, so I walked out and looked for a place to eat. To my surprise I found an Indian vegetarian restaurant, and had a good Indian dinner.

Next morning I left for London, and I got through Customs without a problem, since I was a transit passenger and I spent the night at a nearby hotel. Next day while waiting for my BOAC flight, an air lines employee approached me and asked where I was going? I said New York. He said do you have your medical documents with you? I said yes, they are in my luggage, which was already loaded on the plane. He then looked at my ticket and led me to the plane where he made one of the porters bring down my suitcase so that I could retrieve my documents. That demonstrated how strict the U.S. immigration was at the time. My clear chest x-ray enabled me to enter the country.

What a contrast to present day Immigration check points. Just a few days ago a U.S. citizen, a multiple drug resistant Tuberculosis patient passed through the Canadian border, and was not stopped, even though his condition was noted in the computer. It looks to me as if the U.S. is becoming like a third world country, with sophistication. When we can't stop a guy who knows how to manipulate the system, how are we controlling the so called "Terrorists"? That guy in London alerted me about the medical documents, without those, U.S. Immigration would have turned me back to India, or it would have taken a lot of time to get through the process, and I would have missed my TWA flight to Ohio.

New York Air port, now JFK was so big and fresh looking; I was just awed by it.

People were quite friendly and welcomed us foreigners. Then I went to the TWA terminal, which was wall to wall red, carpeted, as if we were all big dignitaries. Since the Carter administration's air lines travel deregulation, traveling by air is not much fun. I took my short flight to Columbus and felt I finally had landed in the USA.

As I came out of the plane I met the Professor, who welcomed me with folded hands, Indian style Namaste. I felt quite at home seeing him, and while I glanced at a few Indian people including a woman, I walked off with the Professor. Besides those people did not say anything to me as to why they were there. Later I understood they were advised by the International student's office about my coming, but the rumor was that I walked off with a mysterious looking man. I traveled for the first time in a huge, very comfortable American car, an Oldsmobile.

I still could not believe that I was in the USA, and that I was at least going to stay here for three years. The first few days I was put up in the College of Nursing school dormitory temporarily. The Professor tried to make me as comfortable as he possibly could. He took me out to a restaurant where he suggested I select fried chicken and sherbet etc, which he thought will be palatable to my taste. As I settled down in my room I slept to combat my jet lag. The next few days were spent looking for a place to live. The graduate dorm was booked, so my alternatives were to rent an apartment or going to a rooming house, which were registered with the university housing department. I did not like the idea of renting or of going to a rooming house. Lastly, the professor suggested that I go to an undergraduate dorm if it was available, for one quarter only and he was willing to arrange for that. The under graduate dorms were not open to graduate students. I thought it was a brilliant idea because the dorm will provide me with a room, bath room facilities and three meals a day. This arrangement was for a quarter only, during which time I would have learnt my way around. I took his suggestion to be in an undergraduate dorm, with all kinds of white girls, a lot younger than I was; thus started the Americanization process for me.

My Student Life in the USA

At the dorm, I had a single bed, a small desk and a closet. It was sufficient for me to begin student life in the mid- western state of Ohio. I also had three meals at the dorm cafeteria. I was amazed by the abundance of food, prepared and unprepared, arranged neatly on display, and we chose what we wanted to eat. Beef, pork, occasionally chicken and on Friday's fried fish was available, in addition to vegetables, salads, breads and rolls. Milk was plentiful, and dispensed like water from a big container. It was the biggest culture shock and sometimes I felt sad comparing the food to what it was in India. I thought we Indians worshipped the goddess of wealth, Laxmi. Those days, people looked very healthy, not overweight compared to Indian people. Of course, this is changing, as the country's population is becoming obese; that is what I observe after 45 years. There is also an explosion of fast foods; MacDonald's, Kentucky fried chicken Wendy's, doughnut shops and many other supply prepared food 24 hours a day. I did not grow up eating meat as the main dish, and I stayed away from eating beef. In a letter to my grandma I wrote about this beef eating custom, her answer to me was plain and simple- go ahead and eat it, it is their food. But somehow I stayed away from beef. I will be lying if I say I never ate beef, I did, perhaps twice, whereas Indian vegetarian men start eating beef soon after arriving in the USA. In my department, an Indian gentleman told me he does not eat beef, but he ate hamburgers because it is made of Ham. I knew hamburger was not Ham but was beef, and I told him so. He was quite surprised to learn that, but it was late for him to change because he depended too much on hamburger and fries every day; it was convenient for him. I must say food was a bit tasteless but wholesome, and I gained a few pounds very soon.

The university was soon to start fall quarter, and I paid my tuition for about 20 units, enough to keep me busy but to have time to do part of the research job that paid me about $250.00 a month. That was enough to pay my room, food and other expenses beginning next quarter. The current rate, as I learned recently in San Francisco from a graduate student, is about $3000.00 a month. That shows the amount of inflation in about 45 years.

I walked through that huge campus, to go to different departments and the campus was beautiful. The buildings were huge, ivy covered, occupying almost a block. All that walking was making my feet hurt. In India, I used my bicycle or rickshaws, and I did not even have proper footwear. However, the graduate education was so well thought out that my health was covered in the fees I paid. I was not aware of that and one day Professor saw me limping; when I told him all that walking was hurting my feet, he sent me to a podiatrist at the student's health center. The doctor told me that because of my weak arches, I was having this problem. He gave me a prescription for arch supports and said to use Dr. Scholl's footwear. I did obtain a pair but it was not a good looking pair of shoes, and did not go well with my sari outfit, but it helped my walking, which was a big help.

My life in the dorm was not exciting, because as a graduate student I was not a participant in their activities. But I watched how these young ladies lived. They would be quiet and study for the week and then they enjoyed their weekends going on dates or visiting or just simply having a relaxed good time. Friday and Saturday nights I would hear young men singing or serenading out side the rooms. Occasionally girls would stop by to visit with me, most of the time out of curiosity, but we would end up discussing all sorts of topics, including my forehead dot or Bindi as it is called in India. Incidentally I discontinued wearing Bindi, to avoid questions.

We also talked about the newly- elected, President Jack Kennedy. Who would know then that the charismatic leader and President of the country would be gunned down next year? I felt that his wife Jackie was more popular than her husband. Women liked her fashion. Her Pill box hat became a must item in the wardrobe. Also, I learned that JFK was not as popular in the U.S. as he was overseas, that he was an Irish Catholic, elected for the first time by a very narrow margin. They were quite surprised that a catholic was elected in a Protestant country. Fast forward. In 2007, Rudy Giuliani, an Italian American catholic, ex Mayor of New York city is running for President, and he invariably leads in polls. If the election takes place now he probably will be elected President. It was unthinkable in the early sixties. But the election will be later in 2008. I must say things are changed, and a woman (Senator Hillary Clinton) and a half black half white man (Sen. Barack Obama) are also running. Any one of them will make history.

Also, we talked about India and the Kashmir situation. I would tell them that unlike Pakistan, which was a Muslim country; India on the other hand was not a Hindu country but a secular democracy. Hindus happen to be the majority population. I did not know how much I got through on that point but I liked having those dialogues with them. I felt these American female students were quite interesting and I had fun knowing them.

I started my classes, which was not easy for me; I had not sat in a class as a student for almost 10 years. The teaching methodology was also very different. The students interrupted the teachers if they did not understand. It was quite in contrast with teaching in India. The teachers gave quizzes every so often, graded and saved all the grades for final tally for a grade. Final exam for each course was a very informal affair, but a grade of each course was put together for final pass/ fail grading of A through D, and beyond that was a failed grade. I worked hard to get good grades in my courses, for if I did not make good I would be sent home. What a shameful situation that would have been.

I had a desk as my office in a laboratory adjacent to the Professor's office. I shared my lab/office with an American guy, who was a very nice, friendly fellow. Indians were not unknown foreigners and there was quite a tradition of Indian students in the department where they were regarded well, scholastically. Most of the Americans were white guys, and one was a woman. There was one black guy from Texas, and a Rhodesian, who was brought in by the Professor, an Egyptian from Alexandria, who was a friendly guy. Later Thai and Singapore ladies joined the department. The Texan was on the phone a lot of the time. As graduate students, we did not have individual phone lines. There were about four phones in different rooms, which sometimes caused lines to use the phone. I overheard the Texan talking about what was going on in the Black communities in the country. Those were the days when the new charismatic black leader Martin Luther King was giving a lot of lectures while he was marching through the South to bring in civil rights changes in the country. I wish I had paid more attention to what MLK was saying. Later, when I was in India I heard the news that he was assassinated, and I was very sad.

The Rhodesian returned after obtaining his PhD degree, and he became his country's Education Minister. We were friendly, but I lost track of Peter in due time. My quarter was coming to a close, and I was feeling more at ease in my student life in a far away not so strange country. I received letters from home regularly, and I wrote back regularly. Sometimes I missed my family very much, particularly during Indian holidays.

I remember my first Seminar when I did the talking for half an hour or so, followed by questions and answers. It was the Professor's favorite time with the graduate students. There was a tape recorder recording the Seminar every time we met. I was very nervous presenting my topic and after it was over and I faced all the questions but I was not happy with how it went for me. We were graded on how we did and I was not used to this kind of Seminar presentation. When I returned to my office the Professor asked me to go to the Seminar room and listen to the tape. I felt quite awful after I listened to my presentation. I told myself; definitely I will do better the next time. My next seminar was considerably better, and I knew that. The modern technology utilized in teaching was new to me.

Sports are a big thing in these Universities. Of all the sports, football is the most watched and enjoyed sport which is played between Universities with gusto. Each university team has a name and at the end of the season the best two teams play in prestigious tournaments. One is the Rose Bowl, which is played in Pasadena, California on New Years day. I was impressed by the sports including Football in the USA. In India people do not play. There is no sports organization to determine which University is good in any type of sport. I probably am repeating myself if I write that in India this lack of competitive sports, which occurs every four years when the World meets to compete in various sports in the Olympics, seldom results in India being featured.

I do not know why some of the Indian universities do not plan competitions throughout India. I think it is doable and needs some coordination. But the Indian attitude that "it can not be done" prevails, instead of "can do".

Football, USA style, as I came to know is very different from football or Soccer as it is known to the rest of the world. US football is played with a funny looking ball, which is not the usual round shape and is carried by players running to the end of the field to score, while the opposing team tries to stop them the only time they kick the ball is when they are making extra points by a "field goal". This is a very crude way to describe the game as I tried to understand it. I went to see one of those games to get to know the game. I purchased a ticket and climbed a lot of steps to my seat, which was "way up there". It was in a huge stadium of 40,000 seats, the kind I had never seen before in my life. The player's from two different teams, (different universities) were very well built men in game uniforms of two different colors representing their universities. Their heads were protected by helmets and during the half- time, pretty girls in very short outfits entertained with very good gymnastic floor exercises.

After that trip to the football game, I did not go back again, because I wanted to see other games such as Basket ball, Ice hockey etc. Besides, I felt American football was too physical. I only watch the Super Bowl final now for all the hoopla associated with that special game and the Rose Bowl if my University is a finalist playing in that event.

This university also had a beautiful, big auditorium, where they had some good musical programs which I attended once in a while. I was getting used to western music, though slowly. I also went to the movies to see the recent releases, which I did not have the opportunity to do in India.

I ate all the American food, which took some getting used to; however, once in a while I craved some spicy Indian food. I did not cook, and I did not have many Indian friends, except for an Indian woman who was a student, ahead of me by two years. She had already finished her course requirements and was going ahead with her research requirements. She held a technical assistantship with the department. She was a good student and often visited with the Professor for chats or consultations. The Professor had a high regard for her. She always dressed in saris and looked nice; her husband was also a graduate student in another city. She lived with an Indian family, who were also students in other departments. Sometimes, she invited me to have dinner with her, and I always accepted happily. She was a vegetarian. I should write about this person who became a life-long friend of mine. She had a similar background to mine and was teaching in a college back in India, There, a fellow Professor fell for her and they were married. After getting married, they decided to postpone having a family and to go abroad and get their PhDs. They arrived in the U.S. and both of them got their degrees. I do not remember the time line, but he accepted a job in the state of New York and she followed him there. I lost track of her for a few years, then I heard from her that she had had a baby girl, which was good. She was a good mother, and now this girl is an accomplished physician, with a specialty in neurology. However, my friend was satisfied as a wife, mother and now a grandmother. But because of circumstances, she could not utilize her educational background in a meaningful way. An American woman with that background would think of some thing to do even if she did not go to an 8 to 5 job. We visited each other several times, and now we compare notes by telephone on how we are coping with our advancing age.

My first quarter was coming to end, and it was November, I was so thrilled to see my first snowfall and a month before I saw, for the first time the beautiful Fall, when the trees changed colors to different shades of red and yellow as the days were getting cooler. I went shopping for some winter wear such as a heavy coat and stockings etc. I had never seen a department store before, and I was awestruck to see the amount of ready made garments displayed under one big roof. There was no shopkeeper showing his/her goods, instead one walked around looking for the right thing. I was not a good shopper then, and even now I am not a good shopper. My friends know that, so when there is a birthday or some such occasion when a gift is in order, I end up giving a check or a gift certificate. I must say, I like some of the gifts that my friends bring me and I am jealous that they are such good imaginative shoppers. My little sister is a good shopper. She spends hours looking around comparing things, and then returns empty handed, but she knows where to go when she decides on something.

I was looking forward to a four days week end. Americans celebrate Thanksgiving, every year on the fourth Thursday of November. I loved the concept of this holiday. It is nothing to do with any religious connotation, as the holidays are in India. Professor explained to me what this holiday was all about and that on this Thursday Americans of every kind and religion give thanks for their good life. The Pilgrims started the tradition to occur at some date between September 21 and November 9. The date of Thanksgiving was first started by President Lincoln to correlate with the landing of the Mayflower at Cape Cod, Massachusetts on Nov. 21 1620. The fourth Thursday of November was set later by President Franklin D. Roosevelt in 1939, and approved by congress in 1941.

Again, I was impressed by how organized this country is. Of course, I learnt the negative side of this too, i.e., KKK, (Ku Klux Klan) an organization that was based on religious, race hatred was formed in 1866 to maintain white race supremacy.

The International Students office was organized in such a way that every new student went with an American family for Thanksgiving dinner. I was looking forward to meeting the family who had invited me through the International Student's office. Martha and her husband John were on time to pick me up at my dorm. She was a red headed woman with a very pleasant smile and her husband was a friendly, but tough- looking man, both I presumed in their forties. All three of us went by their huge station wagon, an American made car. Americans did not drive small cars then. There was no such a thing as a Toyota or a Nissan. When we got to their place after a 20 miles drive through stretches of almost wilderness and met their two kids, a girl and a boy, the girl was a teenager, a pretty one and friendly looking like her mama. The boy was also a very good looking young fellow. Martha's mother who lived nearby joined us, and after the introductions we started our Thanksgiving dinner.

The main part of this dinner was a big turkey, stuffed with all kinds of stuffing, called dressing, served as a side dish, gravy, cranberry sauce, and cooked green vegetables, mashed potato, a salad, rolls and butter followed by different kinds of pies. John carved the turkey, and took out chunks of white and brown meats to serve at the dinner table. The dinner table was laid out properly, and decorated for Thanksgiving with dried fruits and flowers etc. I was thinking that if this kind of dinner in its finery was showed in an ordinary home, then what would it be like in rich people's homes ? These people were ordinary working class, but Martha had a certain aristocratic style. She even sent a report of my visit to the local newspaper, in which she wrote about me, where I was from etc. Years letter, when I visited them, her kids showed me the newspaper clipping that she had saved. Martha was a very special person in my life then, and 45 years later she still is. But now she is bedridden and living her last days. She was proud to be a descendant of the first settlers and still a paid member of the "Daughters of the American revolution" organization. Her husband was, a rugged looking man of German background. They visited me many times in my various homes in southern California. Sometimes, they even helped paint the whole outside of my house, I bought the paint and brushes and of course I cooked some meals. I learnt from them some of the mixed drinks, I still remember we enjoyed *Harvey wall banger* in Chicago, where I went to attend a meeting, and they joined me there. After spending the night together Martha and John brought me back to my dorm. With that my first Thanksgiving had ended. I will be writing more about Martha later.

I prepared for the finals to end my first quarter. The examination for each course was given by the instructors and very informal compared to examinations given in India. I was taking about four courses. I made all "A" grades, it was a perfect 4 points result and I was sure to continue my studies. This was my first Christmas in the USA, and every thing looked so festive, plus religious music was piped in the dorm and else where. The students at the dorm were packing to go home. I did not know what their grade averages were. We just greeted good byes and merry Christmas. Close to Christmas it was customary to greet with merry Christmas to whom ever you come across on the road or in the department. We do not have this sort of friendliness back home. I was supposed to vacate the dorm by the end of the quarter, but before I left a dear friend of mine, a Philosophy Professor from Varanasi, came to visit me as my guest. My dorm Warden arranged for a bunk bed in my room. My friend stayed with me for two to three days. She was in the U.S. on a visiting Professor's program. It was very nice of my U.S.

Professor to take us to dinner one evening. We spent hours talking about our respective experiences in the U.S. After she left, I started thinking about my next residence. International student's office suggested that I go to a rooming house; they are economical and are under the care of the University housing authorities, so they had to follow rules and regulations laid down by the housing authorities. I consulted with the Professor, and he thought it was an excellent idea to go to a rooming house. In this country most major universities publish a newspaper giving all the news pertinent to students. They also list rooms available in different houses. I selected the homes close to the department, for I did not have any transportation. The Professor suggested that he do the calling to the House mother. I thought just as well, and he did. I got a room at a rooming house about three blocks from my department, and I went there and saw the house and met the young lady, the House mother. The room rent was charged upfront for the quarter. I had enough money saved then from my research assistantship. I had to be frugal, for my monthly stipend was only $250.0 a month. I decided to come to live in that house after the New Year.

We had our departmental Christmas party at the Professor's house which was arranged by his senior students. They arranged some party games such as Charades and a pot luck dinner with every body bringing a dish. I made some *samosas* to take; which; they liked. There were varieties of food from Egyptian casserole to American meatballs. There were all kinds of Christmas cookies and cakes, and it was a pleasant evening. Outside it was snowing, and another thing that impressed me was how they had controlled the indoor temperature, and that is one of the many bench marks as to why we are a third world country.

I left by bus for Iowa to spend my Christmas holidays with my friends. This is a couple, I knew from back home where she was teaching at the same college with me, and her husband was in another college. In the U.S., she was doing her PhD degree, and he was a post doctoral Fellow. They had two little kids and I had a very pleasant visit with them. She was a mother, a wife and a graduate student all put together, a low- keyed personality, who always got the job done. When I first came to know her, she was a single lady and teaching, while helping her brother and sister through college. She was quite a bit senior to me, therefore, held a seniority aura, and I respected her. She fell in love with a younger man, who was doing his graduate studies in another college. There was quite a bit of rumor mill operating for that, and she stopped the entire rumor and announced her wedding. I was an invited guest at their wedding. Soon after, they left for the U.S. for higher studies. At their place in Iowa, I ate a lot of Indian food, and talked all about our respective student lives and I rested a lot, because I did have a very hectic life. After completing their studies they left for India. I shall write about them when I too return to India. I took the bus ride back to my place. This was a 17-18 hours long bus ride, and a boring one to say the least, most of the travel was at night with nothing much to look at. In the morning also, there was no scenery but vast stretches of flat farm lands, in short the mid -west was not much to look at. Upon my return I was ready to begin my second quarter. As I look back now I do not think I can even consider about taking such a grueling trip by bus. I am thankful that airlines connect this vast country every which way you want to go. But the Bus ride is relatively cheaper and at the time suited my pocket book.

Life with the Americans

I started the winter quarter and the New Year in my new address at the rooming house. The Professor had given me a ride, and we were introduced to the young lady, the house mother, who was known as Mrs. D. It was one of the very pleasant experiences for me to live in a rooming house. Even though the students were all undergraduates as in the dorm, they probably were not so well off financially. There were ten of us in the house. This was an old two story Victorian house, fixed up to be a rooming house. There were ten rooms, but only one bath room on the second floor. Lucky for me, I had a small wash basin in my room. Now a days the new houses have more bathrooms than rooms. We did not have a kitchen, but in the basement there was a small kitchen facility, with a hot plate and a refrigerator. The house mother, a young lady, and her husband lived in the basement apartment. After the Professor left and I checked into my room, she invited me for a get together chat over a cup of coffee. She was a very pretty petite woman from the south, and I could tell her from her southern accent. We became friends instantly; she was about two years younger than I. She told me rather innocently that had I called her to rent the room instead of the Professor calling, she would have rejected me for my foreign accent. She said she would have told me the room is already rented. Then she said she did not rent to Blacks, Asians etc even though it was unlawful to refuse based on ethnicity. She also did not care to rent to a Jew. She had the notion that those people do not keep their rooms clean. Therefore, the Professor's call for me was the testament as a reference that I would be a good addition to her house. She was also impressed, because I was a graduate student from India. She was an English major and junior (third year college) at the University. She, with the help of her husband, kept the place spick and span, they were a very hard- working couple. He had a job at the local research institute. One by one I came to know all the girls, who were a friendly bunch, but they all disliked the lady, because she always checked the rooms every morning and would write up, if the room did not look neat to her. She had the authority to throw us out of the house if she found us not desirable. She would come to my room often just to visit, and the girls were curious about it. We could tell if Mrs. D was coming or going by her foot steps.

She always made a cake and celebrated every ones' birth day when she would bring out her beautiful Rosenthal China set. She told me they bought the set when her husband was stationed in Germany, in the armed forces. Sometimes she stopped by to complain about the girls, such as the Jewish girl, Bobby, who lived across from my room. Mrs. D thought she fed a stray cat in her room, and she did not like that and she wanted to stop that. I was quite friendly to Bobby, and I alerted her about the cat. She had the largest room, or the most expensive one. She was a very nice, pretty girl, and contrary to my opinion that all Jewish people are very good in studies, she was not, she barely made C or D grades, however, she did graduate eventually with teaching credentials .She came from a rich family. Her father owned super market chains. She invited me to her home, which I did visit. Her parents were very hospitable; they gave me their bed room for the couple of days that I spent with them. Bobby graduated after two quarters.

I learnt about eating Pizza at the rooming house. One day, one of the girls came and asked me if I would split a Pizza, I did not know what she was talking about. She then explained to me that they were calling to have a Pizza delivered and would I share with them and divvy up the cost. I said yes, and learnt about Pizza. I enjoyed the Pizza very much, and I told them to count me in next time they ordered Pizza.

That quarter Mrs. D. was taking some courses and she had to tackle Logic, which she found needed some interpretation. She approached me to help her, and I used my scientific knowledge to interpret inductive and deductive logic for her, and I thought she was happy with my help. One of the girls who used to be very critical of the house mother was Linda. She would always mimic her southern accent, and even questioned her intelligence. In spite of her criticism of Mrs. D, we became very good friends, and our friendship endured many years. She was another very gorgeous looking girl with style. She was also renting one of the larger, better furnished rooms. She was studying for her dental hygienist certificate, which took about two years. The girls would come to her on Fridays and Saturdays to ask her help with the hair styling and dressing before going out. She was going steady with a guy and in those days dating was quite a formal affair, and the guys did not expect any thing more after paying for a dinner at a restaurant. I could make out next morning how the date went for these girls. I would compare this with our girls back home, who would be presented to the guy and his family to check out if she was acceptable for a marriage proposal. This has not changed much in India. At the end of the quarter, Linda broke up with her boy friend, she became quite sad, but bounced back and finished her studies. I did not know the guy, but I did not care for him.

I was very busy as usual with my studies, research job, and library work etc. I was a career driven person, and I knew if I did not do well, I would have to go home. I took a full load of courses so that I could finish my course requirements soon and concentrate on my research.

74

One evening as I was busy in my lab trying to prepare some culture plates my sari caught fire and so also did my long hair; however, I was prepared for such a catastrophe, thanks to my NCC training. I fell to the ground and rolled myself, and that extinguished the fire, and saved another of my many lives. Since it was winter time, I covered the burnt sari with my long coat and walked home.

Linda used to be my friend at the house and I enjoyed talking to her. She was nine years younger than I was, but she was much mature compared to other girls. One day as I was fixing some food in the basement, Linda came in and she asked me "what are you doing" I said I am cooking a chicken curry, an Indian dish. She said I could smell that, I felt bad that the smoke from my cooking was bothering her but she said she liked it and therefore, came down to check it out. I then invited her to share my chicken and rice dinner. She ate this kind of spicy food for the first time and fell in love with it. I did not cook Indian food a lot; I cooked only when I craved for some spicy food. Besides, I did not want the house to get that Indian food aroma, which lingers on. We became good friends and I learnt about U.S. customs, politics, food etc from her, and she learnt about my religion and India. I often wondered if her vast general knowledge was the reason why she did not go on dates a lot. I felt men do not like knowledgeable girls, who express themselves intelligently. Occasionally, her mother drove down with her son, Linda's younger brother, to visit with her. Sometimes when I opened the door to let them in, she whispered to me to find out if Linda goes out on dates or not. I would say I do not know who she goes out with. Incidentally, she had broken up with the guy she was going with. She was a bit sad, so I had introduced her to Basil, a Welch guy who had joined our group.

One of the girls named Martha, who was getting married, invited me and a few other girls including Linda to her marriage. I wanted Linda to help me with my hair style. I do not think she had handled long hair before, she asked me why we do not cut the hair short. I agreed to her suggestion, because I was finding long hair a little inconvenient in the winter time. This was the first time my long hair was gone, and my hair was collected by Bobby who was going to make a braid out of it to wear. I attended an American church wedding for the first time. It was a very orderly and presentable service. Martha walked with her father in a beautiful wedding gown. Wedding vows were short as was the exchange of rings. The priest said a prayer and the wedding was over, followed by a reception, in contrast to Indian weddings, where so much goes on. Indian weddings look festive in a chaotic way. Nevertheless, it was a good experience for me. Martha gave me a set of her wedding pictures, which I still have.

Another girl I still remember from the house was Lynn; she was an energetic, woman and a very religious one. Her room was adjacent to mine, and she would pop in once in a while, and try to learn about my religious upbringing. When she learned I was not a Christian, she felt pretty bad for my soul. She brought me a lot of Christian literature, and suggested that I go with her to one of Billy Graham's lectures. He was one of the up and coming evangelists at the time. He is quite old now, but he had been friends of many Presidents up to the present President. I never attended the lectures, because I had no religious needs. I was happy occasionally repeating my mantra that provided me with my inner peace. Lynn gave up working on me, besides, she had a lot of trouble at home, I do not remember the details but she left the house. She was the only one I met with such strong religious beliefs.

Those were cold winter days, so I would return home to avoid walking alone at night from the department. Sometimes, I used to entertain myself by palm reading. All the girls were interested to know their future including Mrs. D. I had started this palm reading when I was undergoing military training for NCC. I read some books, before going to the training camp and thought I would get to look at so many hands of women unknown to me, for practice. I was quite surprised that some of them believed me, including Linda and Mrs. D. I will tell how much they believed in my palm reading later.

I was leading a different life at the department, and I would leave that life there before returning to my room, so girls, though curious, did not know my other life.

I was working hard, took some tough courses, and kept up with my research work. I began to see some patterns in the research that Professor suggested which was to write an abstract to present at a scientific meeting to be held in Amherst, Mass. I was quite excited with the prospect that I will be presenting my research in front of a research community for the first time in my life. So I started to put my data together. The Professor was very helpful in my endeavour. He was also helpful in ways hard to describe, for instance I had to walk about a mile to go to a class in a far away building in the morning in winter time, after the class I would be out in the cold again to walk back to my department. Suddenly I would see a familiar car stopping and asking me if I need a ride. Guess who that was? I had such rides quite a few of those winter days, and I appreciated each one of them. At night when I was ready to leave the department, suddenly the Professor would appear and ask me if I need a ride home. How could I refuse such help? I wanted to do something to show my appreciation, so behind the scenes; I worked for him to get the year's best prestigious teaching award. I thought he deserved it, and some one had to nominate him for consideration. This was a token of appreciation for his help to me, every step of the way. I got together with another graduate student; I knew who was one of the Professor's favorites. One day I acquired a list of all his ex-graduate students from his office, which was open to us, and passed it on to that guy. He wrote a general letter to all those people to request them to vote him the best Professor of the year. He was quite surprised when his name was announced, and he was communicated by the awarding committee for an award ceremony. His picture was the front page in our university newspaper and maganazine. Mrs. D, my house mother wanted an autograph on one of those pictures, so I brought her to my department to give her his signature which she was happy to receive.

While all this was happening, I felt a certain subtle relationship was building up, which I did not feel comfortable He was 25 years older than I, and I found out that he was a married man. So "what kind of a scenario" am I looking at was my thought? In the meantime my friend from Iowa decided to be a matchmaker for me and made arrangements for me to meet an Indian Doctor, in Chicago halfway from Iowa. I accepted her offer and decided to go to Chicago over the weekend. I told the Professor I will be out of town. He sensed that some thing was going on, but did not ask any questions. I took a bus to Chicago, which was about a 10 hour's journey by Greyhound bus. Such long distance buses are so comfortable; in India I would not think of such a long bus journey, I arrived in the morning and I met the guy at a predetermined site. I was in my sari outfit so it was not hard for him to find me. This man was ok, and had a MD degree from India, and worked for a Veterans Administration hospital. But something was not clicking with me and my gut feeling was that may be I did not want to get married after all, also I was comparing this man with the polished behavior of the Professor. This man was looking for a girl to get married. I told him I will stay in touch, and left Chicago, end of the story. The Doctor, I understood married later a Phillipina nurse and I am sure that he lived a happy married life. My friend in Iowa was very unhappy with me, because I let the Doctor slip away. At least one load off my shoulder. I got back to my routine soon after I returned. I spent that Thanksgiving with my new friend Linda instead of going to Martha, where I went for my first Thanksgiving. Just a few days before Thanksgiving President Kennedy was assassinated in Dallas, Texas. It was a very sad day, and we were glued to the television set. Amazing how well they do things on TV. Jackie, the tower of strength, walking in the funeral procession, all played on the television.

My Thanksgiving with Linda and her family was very enjoyable. Her mother was a very good cook, and made the usual elaborate dinner. I also met her granny, who was a German immigrant an independent-woman. Linda had very high regard for her. She reminded me of my granny, but they were two different people. I met her other relatives also and Linda told me how conservative her father was. After my visit I returned home and finished my fall quarter, then started the winter quarter.

Winter quarter was coming to an end, and I was preparing for my examinations. All the girls were arranging to go home during the quarter break, and Mrs. D and her husband were also heading south to Tennessee for the break, I did not know what I was going to do. I had a dear friend in Chicago who was living with her family; we were friends in India, and colleagues. She had invited me to visit her, so I called her to say I would like to come to visit her. She was very happy to hear from me and I decided to go there. They had three little girls. Her husband was a brilliant scientist, and worked in Chicago, at a prestigious institution at the time. I had very high regards for his brilliant scientific mind, but I did find him a bit of a flirt. Perhaps some men read single women differently, but it was manageable, and I had a good visit with them and left Chicago as my quarter break ended. So this was my second trip to Chicago shortly after the first one. When I was leaving for Chicago, I was the last one to leave the house that afternoon. My house mother had turned off the heater before she left in the morning. By the time I was leaving, the house was extremely cold and I had never felt as cold before I was shivering. I can see the difference in how they have improved the way they insulate the houses now; heat holds like a thermos flask does.

I received my result in the mail. It was good again, and I felt quite secure as a graduate student. I started my spring quarter with a heavy load of courses again. My paper was accepted, and a group of us along with the Professor attended the meeting in Massachusetts. I was happy with my presentation.

Mrs. D made my birthday cake, a red velvet cake, and all of us gathered and had a pleasant time together. The spring quarter also ended successfully. Most of the students took off for the summer as the house was quite empty, as was the department. I registered for the quarter to collect some credits for doing full time research. The Professor gathered some of us foreign students and a few Americans to go to the play ground for a base ball game. I had never seen a baseball game before, so it was interesting to learn to play it. I was getting my letters from home regularly and I kept them posted as to what ever I was doing, they were counting the days for my return. I felt very home sick when ever I got a letter from home.

We were starting fall quarter again but my life was becoming complicated. One day the Professor asked me out to dinner, this time no one else was going with us. We went to a very good restaurant; generally he invited one or two other students but this time no one but me. We had a very good dinner. He had a cocktail prior to the main meal, and I drank my water. When he was dropping me off he kissed me. I was surprised, and asked what was that for? Then I left. That night I had a restless night, I was wondering how I was supposed to handle the situation. Moreover, I was never kissed by a man before;

of course I had a soft spot for him. I was thinking of an episode which was playing out in my mind, which happened a few years earlier when I was doing my graduate work and living at my parents. One day my father came and told us that his friend's daughter brought shame to him, because she, a married woman with children eloped with an older person, a renowned movie Director from abroad. This lady was also married to a movie Director, and lived next door to the visiting foreigner. I had seen her picture in the news papers. My father was very sad for his friend, so how could I do any thing that would be very much detrimental to my father's thinking?

Next morning, I got myself together and went to the department and straight to his office. I said I want to talk with you, and then he shut the door and sat me down, and went on to say that he did not know why I took it so bad. I said you know I come from a different culture, and it is not possible for me to handle a thing on the side and carry on with my studies, research etc. It is not right.

Finally, he said let us talk about it sometime later, and I left his office. I was very stressed out. There was no where to go for me for counseling, and I did not want to hurt him either. I considered him a friend and a mentor. The last alternative, to pack up and go home, was not quite what I would have liked to do; I wanted to finish my degree. I decided to ask him if it was possible for me to take my qualifying examination, part written and part oral given by a committee, and in the event I pass I could start doing my research to complete my PhD requirements sooner. He as my adviser, therefore, was to arrange that examination. When I finally got around to talking to him about my idea to hasten my examination, he said he will look into it; he knew I was not very happy. He left town and I did not know what was going on as we were not talking much.

After a few days when he returned, we had our regular research group meeting. After that, it was lunch time and he asked me if I was free to join him for lunch, and I said yes. At the lunch we talked mostly about my comprehensive examination. He said I do have enough course credits to go for the exam, and that beyond the course knowledge, some of the committee members have a tendency to drift to other general knowledge questions at the oral examination. Are you prepared for such cross questioning? He was not sure who would be my committee members; he said he will decide about that. Then he proceeded to tell me that I would be happy to learn that he had accepted a position to go to Brazil on an educational mission on leave from the university, and it may take more than a year to complete his job, but he will leave after I finish my comprehensives. I still could carry on with the financial support with his research grant, which he said will be active for the duration. Furthermore, he also talked about his life and his relationship with the lady in his house, and I would like to keep his secret. I was, sincerely very happy with the turn of the situation. We finished our lunch and returned to the department. He then announced to his group his plans about his new assignment abroad. He had decided to take his favorite American graduate student with him to assist him with his job, and he could complete his studies at the university there.

Completing My Degree

This will be the beginning of the end of my graduate degree. While I was happy that I did not have to take the one sided approach by the man responsible for my stay at the department, I was feeling sad that he will be leaving shortly, because, as I said earlier I did have a soft spot for him. My first order of business was to get myself prepared for the exam, and next order of business was to select my research advisor to replace the Professor. I decided on two Professors jointly as my advisors to replace the Professor, and my selection was acceptable to him. I was studying hard. At the rooming house the girls knew I was studying for some big examination, so they stopped popping in to visit with me. I still was going to the department to do my research job, and once in a while the Prof. gave me a ride back home. During one of those rides back he told me he did care for me and he will be looking forward to know my progress via letters while he was gone, and that he will attend my graduation commencement.

My written examination was given by three different Professors, which I finished on three different days, and waited for my results. When the reports came that I passed my written part, I was given my oral exam date. In the mean time, I was feeling a bit neglected because Mrs. D did not arrange the cake-coffee get together for me on my birth day. She knew my examination days, however. My oral was one evening starting at 6 PM to 9 PM. That evening, I took a deep breath and said my mantra and went to take my exam. The exam was given in the seminar room, where 5 professors attended and Prof. was the head of the committee to test my ability academically, and enable me to finish the program. After two hours of grueling questioning the last question was who did I think was the most important man in this century. I thought he was looking for Einstein as the answer, but I was wrong; he was looking for Mahatma Gandhi as my answer. After that my oral examination was history, and years later Time magazine made Einstein that man followed by Gandhi. I was told to wait in my office for the result. Shortly after the Prof. walked in, shook my hand and told me I passed my oral. I was overjoyed and started to walk home but he gave me a ride. As I was leaving he kissed me again and said it was for my success, I was too happy and did not seem to mind at that point.

When I arrived home, as I opened the door suddenly all those women shouted happy birthday and each came and gave me a hug, and there was Mrs.D's red cake and coffee. She told me that she delayed this because she did not want to disturb me while I was getting ready for the exam. I thought it was so thoughtful of her. We had a good time and I told them that I passed my examination. I wanted to take a couple of days off to relax but I did not know where to go, so I started my research towards finishing my degree with the new advisers. At that get together the house mother also announced that she was planning to close down the rooming house and she gave notice to find other places to live. Linda was returning home to start her dental job. Mrs. D's husband Bill was moving to Washington DC with a transfer job and she was to join him as soon as she completed her degree.

I started looking around for accommodation starting with the summer quarter. The girl from Singapore in our department was living in an efficiency apartment not too far from the department, and her room mate, another girl from Singapore had finished her program and gone back home. She would continue for two more quarters. So she asked me if I would like to share with her, and I was very happy to accept her offer. After the end of the quarter I said goodbye to my friends at the rooming house and left. Linda and Barbara (Mrs. D) were the only two women who kept in touch with me.

I did take a few days off to visit the upstate New York Finger Lakes area with my Indian Jewish friend, Leah, who was doing some studies at the university. She told me that she and her departmental secretary, who also was Jewish, were going there and I could join them. I agreed and the lady drove us; it was a good break for me. We stayed in motels and really had a care- free enjoyable time relaxing. Soon after, the professor left for Brazil. Prior to that he invited me for a dinner, and this time I was happy to accept. I wished him well, and he said he will write to me to know how I was progressing.

It took me a little time to get used to the new advisors, but it was working out just fine. I was working hard with my research work and attending seminars. Living with the Singapore girl was satisfactory especially as she cooked most of the time and I shared her food. I learnt Chinese cooking from her. She was a very smart young lady, who was awarded a government scholarship. The following quarter she finished and was ready to return home. I decided to stay on in the apartment without a room mate, and negotiated my rent down with the home owner.

Barbara, Mrs. D my previous house mother who had moved to Washington DC, came to visit me and stayed for a few days. She invited me to visit her in DC.which I did soon after as their house guest. Barbara was then teaching English at a High school in Bethesda. She had to teach a chapter on Gandhi, and she asked me to talk to the students about Gandhi, since he was Indian. I was happy to talk to her students and to prepare for the occasion I went to the Indian Embassy and met the person who was the public relations individual.

It worked out well, because this person was from Varanasi, so we had some common things to talk about. He gave me a documentary film on Gandhi's life, and I thought it will be good to show the film to her students and then answer questions later. Barbara agreed. After the movie I was prepared to answer questions from the students who were from affluent DC families and the adjacent Virginia area. All they wanted to ask me was about India, Pakistan and Kashmir. I had to explain that India was a secular democracy, where every body has equal rights. Those days there was a lot of agitation in Black America, and Martin Luther King and other civil rights leaders were bringing their problems to the fore front. I had learned that Washington DC had a majority black population, so I answered the students with a question: do you think USA should make a separate state for black people in the DC area because the blacks are in the majority? I followed it up with the answer that you do not have to, because you are a democracy. That is the same reason why Kashmir remains in India. I also told them that India has the second largest Muslim population in the world after Indonesia. Barbara then ended the class and thanked me for my participation. I met Barbara's senior English teacher George, an old guy, whom I also noticed was over- attentive to her.

That evening Bill and Barbara took me out to a swanky bar to enjoy the evening, before we went out to dinner. Bill and Barbara took me out sight seeing and I felt that Washington was the most beautiful city, with all those monuments of Washington, Jefferson, and Lincoln as if they are watching over the city and the county for ever. I felt it was a very well planned city. We went to visit the Arlington National cemetery where JFK was laid to rest. There is an eternal flame burning there and I was much moved.

I returned to my work, and received my first of many letters from the Professor, who sounded very happy and upbeat with the challenges he was facing, including learning Portuguese. His letters were very well written and I could read between the lines his feelings for me. Of course he asked me how my research was coming along and as I wanted to hear from him soon I wrote back quickly. I told him how busy I was with my research and that I had some interesting results to report. He replied just as fast and suggested that I start statistical analysis of my data to examine critically. I thought that was a very good suggestion so I started going to the Statistics department to learn some basics of data analysis. I had collected a lot of data and I met with my advisers to determine if it was enough to wrap up my experimental part. My advisers agreed that I could stop my lab work, and take time to analyze data and start writing my dissertation. It was such a liberating feeling that days spending long hours at the lab were over. I wrote a long letter to the Professor to let him know my progress.

I had several meetings with one of my advisers to talk about my experimental results and data analysis and asked him if he agrees with what I was looking at. He agreed with me totally, so I started writing my dissertation or thesis. The writing part was laborious with frequent library consultation. Those days I had to spend long hours going through research abstracts at the library. Now I know how lucky the students are; they can just google it to get their literature search right at their computer terminals. The computer is the name of the game now. I was hand -writing every thing. After I finished writing the Introduction; I gave it to my senior adviser to read. He told me it was coming along all right. This was followed by Literature Review that took a lot of my time at the library.

Linda came to visit me. She was working then, and looked happy with her new Ford Mustang car, and fashionable clothes. She brought me a gift for my pending graduation. I took a couple of days break to spend time with her, and prepared her favorite curry dinner, and then she was gone. I did not see her again until later when I returned as an immigrant. Those days she used to write very good letters, which she discontinued; I do not know why.

Writing my dissertation was progressing well and it looked almost certain that I would be able to meet the dead lines to submit the dissertation, I would be able to go through the last hurdle of defending the research, and finally walk in the commencement procession to receive the degree in person from the chief guest at the ceremony which was to take place at the huge sports stadium.

I found a very good typist to type my manuscript, and after a few changes the rough draft was finalized and she finished the final typing. The cost was $100.00, which I felt was very reasonable. There were no Xerox machines then, so she made four copies on special paper with carbon copiers in between. I kept the last copy with me, for it was the least readable. My oral examination was in the same seminar room, and there were four examiners and a graduate school representative as an observer. The examination went off well, and my senior adviser told me that I passed the exam. It was one of the happiest days of my life. I wrote letters to my family and the Professor to let them know that I had successfully finished my studies, and I was planning to come home.

As promised, Professor came to attend my Commencement; in India they call it Convocation which we inherited from the British, but Americans have to call it differently. My friends John and Martha attended also, so I did not feel lonely. The Professor invited me for dinner and said he was giving me a gift which was a visit to New York City, I was very happy to accept, because I did not know if I would ever visit the largest city ever, after I leave this country. I planned my trip to New York with his return trip to S. America from JFK, which was now the name of New York International Airport. I visited the well known tourist places including the Empire state building and the United Nations building. I felt it was too big a city, and it needs lot more time to get to know the city. I spent some time with the Prof. before he left on his trip back. I felt pleased that our friendship had survived.

My Plans to Return Home

After I returned from New York I wanted to buy my international air ticket home and arrange to ship my things by sea. Martha, my friend was very kind to keep me for a few days while I got ready for my return travel. Some of my Indian friends suggested that I go to the travel agent that they liked, as she did a good job for them. I agreed, and contacted her office. She was a tall slender lady who smoked constantly. She was more manly than feminine, but very good to talk to. I understood she traveled a lot and lived in Europe for a long time and she gave me some ideas that I thought had merit. As per her suggestion I decided to travel by Santa Fe train from Chicago with a stop to visit the Grand Canyon, and take the same train to Los Angeles. My flight from Los Angeles International included sight- seeing stop overs in Honolulu (Hawaii), Hong Kong, Bangkok (Thailand) and on to Calcutta, India. The whole trip sounded very exciting so I finalized my trip with her and paid my bills. The agent told me to keep in touch with her.

Her first name was the same as the Professor's last name, so it was hard to forget her.

I contacted my friend in Chicago and said that I would like to visit her on my return trip to India as I was going to take a train to Los Angeles. She said she will be very happy to see me again. My Honolulu trip was helped by the Professor, whose ex students lived there and held good positions in some of the industries there. He wrote them letters to take care of me as I was returning to India. Every plan was coming along well, and I said good bye to John, Martha and their children Cindy and Steve perhaps for the last time. Then I left for Chicago where I visited my friends. Their three kids were now pretty grown up girls, and they were all very good students. After spending a few days with them, I left for Los Angeles by Santa Fe railways.

My Last Days in the USA as A Student

The Santa Fe train was very different from the trains I was used to. This was a very sleek looking train, with seating arrangement as in the Airlines, no overcrowding as in Indian trains. There was a lounge on the second level, and a dining car. It was three days two nights travel to Los Angeles, with a stop for few hours to visit the Grand Canyon. It was a long cross country journey through the farm lands of this country going through many States. I remember crossing the Mississippi river. At one station the seat next to me which was empty became occupied by a new passenger, an old man. When the train started again, the man introduced himself, and told me that he was 92 years old and said that recently his wife passed away. His kids were giving him this trip, and he may marry again, that was probably what his spouse would have liked; I thought what a difference between him and a ninety year old Indian. I was impressed by his wishes to live his life, and not just wait to die.

I had my dinner at the dinning car which was just like a well- run high- priced restaurant. I was asked to sit with some other people I did not know, and when one of my table mates left, a lady who was waiting for a seat said she wanted to sit next to me, she asked me if I mind? I said no, so she then joined me at the table. She said she spotted me as an Indian woman because of my Sari dress; therefore, she wanted to join me. Then she asked me if I knew an Indian lady whose name she could not pronounce Sarojini, so she wrote it on the napkin. I was very surprised, because the person whose name she wrote was a dear friend of mine at the same university, in a very high position at the Department of Education and quite senior to me. I asked her where she met Sarojini. She met her somewhere in Kansas through her company which she used to ship her belongings to India. They became good friends and she was very happy to meet a friend of a friend. She gave me her address in Los Angeles, where she lived with her business partner and husband. I noted her telephone number and address and told her I would tell my friend Sarojini of this friendly encounter with her friend in a train. We had our short scheduled stop at the famous Grand Canyon Park. I walked up to the south rim observation look out and saw the most spectacular sight. I wished all my relatives were with me to see the view.

I arrived at Los Angeles station, and took a taxi to the Ambassador hotel, in the middle of down town LA. I selected a small, low budget room for a few days. I contacted John who had done his degree ahead of me and settled in Orange County in California, near LA. He knew I was coming, and he had given me his telephone number. Next day, John and his wife came and picked me up at the hotel and took me to Disney Land, which had recently opened. I felt as if I was dreaming: I felt sad for Indian kids, because they do not have anything like it. We need to have a visionary and an achiever like Walt Disney to build a place like that. When we went out to dinner, one could see the difference between mid west and west coast. The population looked mixed with a predominance of Latin Americans, Chinese and other East Asians. The next day I went sight seeing by myself and visited Universal Studios, Hollywood, Beverly Hills etc. and prayed to God that I come back here to live, in short I fell in love with the place. This was one time God had listened to me one hundred percent, because I was back in Los Angeles within four years.

I checked out of the Ambassador Hotel, where Robert Kennedy was shot and killed prior to his nomination as the Democratic Presidential candidate. Now the hotel is gone, and something else has replaced it.

My flight to Honolulu took about five hours, and Hawaii Time is quite a few hours behind west cost time, so I arrived in the middle of the day. I was received Hawaiian style with floral lei (wreath) by Dr. Wismer. He took me to a reasonably priced motel and later in the evening he and his wife took me out for a Luau (Hawaiian dinner). Next day I had dinner at Dr. Anderson's place, regular American food. They were very cordial and friendly people.

Dr. Wismer gave me a tour of Honolulu and it was good, but I told myself, it is not for me, because I felt surrounded by the ocean which was not for me. I did visit the sugar cane and pineapple research stations which were quite interesting. When I was ready to leave town I said goodbye to Dr Wismer and thanked him for his gracious hospitality. I invited him to visit me in India, which he really did a few months later.

Off To Hong Kong. Good Bye to the USA.

Hong Kong, a bustling city, still under British control is an interesting place. I did not do much home work to determine ahead what to see, so I decided to go do my own sight seeing. People in the States had advised me to watch my pocket book all the time; pick pockets are very common there. I took a boat trip to see the city sky line, had a very good Chinese dinner, did some shopping, and I bought a beautiful wrist watch, which was later stolen from my wrist in India at a railway station.

My next stop was Tokyo, Japan. This country had already become an industrial power house. My travel agent had booked me at the Hilton Hotel. I was impressed by the cleanliness of that country. Which also looked to me very homogenous; every body looked Japanese. Every thing was very expensive compared to Hong Kong. I took a tour of the city and after two days stay I was off to Bangkok.

Bangkok in Thailand was not as vibrant as it is today. Then I felt I was in a third world country, people were hustling for my money or the tourist dollars, from getting a hotel room to hiring a Taxi. However, people were very polite and nice and I took a city tour.

Back To India

I was back in Calcutta after thousands of miles, going through different time zones and countries and crossing the International Date Line. I was happy to be back and looking forward to seeing my family.

After visiting my family and recovering from jet lag I went to Varanasi and reported to my job. I did not see much change from the day I left almost three years ago.

I was given temporary accommodation before I was allotted a place and shortly after my arrival, my travel agent lady visited me from the USA. I was very surprised to see her so soon. I went to the airport and picked her up and brought her to the University Guest house as my guest. She said she was on a world tour and thought of looking me up to see how I was doing. I spent a few days with her, since I was not yet teaching. I had some spare time so I showed her Sarnath, which is a few miles from Varanasi, and a Buddhist religious place. She bought some Varanasi silks, and soon went on to continue her World tour. I was happy to see her, but wondered, since I barely knew her, what was the hurry to come to see me? Well, I forgot about her, and concentrated on my settling in.

I was informed by Calcutta Customs that I could come and pick up my trunk that had arrived from the U.S so I decided to go to Calcutta. When I arrived there at the dock, I found that my trunk had been opened and rummaged through, and nothing much was left in it to bring back with me. This was my first disappointment. I reported this theft, which I was told at the dock was quite common, I also reported the loss to the shipping company that shipped my trunk, but as I did not have any sale slips for my things they gave me $200.00 compensation. I was very sad to loose my things, and I was made aware that I was now in a third world country.

I started my work, and instead of utilizing my knowledge and new teaching methodologies for interactive teaching, I reverted back to my old style. I thought students felt comfortable with that. I started receiving nice letters from the Professor, which I answered quickly. That summer there was a summer school organized by our department, jointly with some of the U.S universities. Lo and behold the Professor from the U.S was one of my two advisers. He was quite pleasantly surprised to see me there and I attended some of the sessions given by him. At one such gathering the Head of the Department asked the American professor how "can we implement the American system"? He answered, "You have her, pointing at me. She can help, she came from there". This was the first time I felt gender discrimination. If I were a man and returned with a PhD degree I would have been given a free hand to do things, instead of the way I was treated.

Things did not change much, including my salary, which stayed the same and I was becoming disappointed. In the winter time there was going to be an International Symposium to be held in Delhi. I suggested the Professor attend and present a paper. He accepted my suggestion and decided to send his paper for presentation. To attend the meeting he would be coming all the way from far away Brazil and I also suggested that he come to Varanasi and give a talk at my university. When my department came to know he was going to visit Varanasi, they formally invited him to give a lecture, which he accepted. I was very happy to see him at the air port. I had arranged for his stay at the University guest house. He gave a very good talk to my department and after the lecture he met the head of the department in his office where I joined them. I remember one conversation in which the American Professor asked the Indian professor what is the biggest problem India is facing? The Indian answered that population control is the biggest problem. When the Professor and I returned to the Guest house he asked me how many kids he had, I said more than four I think. He did not ask any more questions. He had only one son.

Professor and I left for New Delhi to attend the International seminar with a stop over at Agra to see the Taj Mahal. This was a very pleasant side trip which I shall not forget. The professor met some of his ex- students in Delhi, who had also come to attend the meeting. After the meeting we said good bye, and I thought this was perhaps my last visit with him, but who knows what the future holds?

I returned to my University, and tried to concentrate on my work and get my living quarters together. I started receiving in quick succession, letters from my new friend, and the Professor's name sake travel agent in the U.S. She was back there after her around- the- world trip. In her letters she started hinting that I should think about immigrating to the USA. I wrote back that, it was not possible because I have to pay back my Study Abroad requirements. Under the agreement I had to stay at my position for four years before I could go abroad, or repay a lump some of money which I did not have. She wrote back that I could return that money with one pay check in the U.S. This sort of correspondence went on for a while, and then she decided to come to visit me again. Well, this time I was not looking forward to her visit. I realized traveling was not very expensive for her, because as a travel agent she was getting discounted fares and the hotels were cheaper too. This time she said that she was traveling prior to her settling down in San Antonio, Texas, where she had a house with a swimming pool. When she arrived, I picked her up, and she stayed with me. She wanted me to travel with her to Delhi, Agra and Jaipur so I went along with her; we stayed in good hotels, courtesy of my travel agent friend.

In Delhi, we went to the U.S. Embassy, and picked up the immigration papers, I went along to satisfy her, as I knew very well that those days immigration was a long- drawn process and that she would stop telling me about immigration. It was not to be. She returned home and soon letters started coming. I could not shut her out either, because, I was not very happy at my job which after almost two and half years did not improve, and I was becoming frustrated, so immigration looked more and more attractive. I also applied for some Post doctoral fellowships in Canada as I thought it was easier to go to Canada. I did get an offer from one of the universities there but I left the offer in my files and wrote them that I would contact them soon.

Immigration was not so easy. I did not have a relative in the U.S., and I had no job lined up there, so the U.S. consulate informed me that my waiting period will be approximately 3 to 5 years. I sent a copy of that letter to my friend. This time she sent me an appointment letter with her travel agency with a salary. She wrote that this will give me priority at the embassy.

I submitted the letter with the application, and waited for the response from the Embassy. There was delay, and then she arranged for a letter written by her Senator to the Embassy, of which I received a copy, I wish I had saved the letter, but I did not. I was sent my visa to go to the USA as an immigrant after only a short wait.

My Return to the USA

It was the peak and valley for me while I got my Immigrant's visa taken care of; I did not know how I was going to get out of my job. Every thing worked out with the help of my mother, and my secretary. I had to give a final practical examination to my students along with an external Examiner. These examinations are very formal affairs in India, and every thing had to be done with utmost care, writing every student grading in three sets, for thirty students. We finished all the obligatory result sheets ready to be sent to the Administrative office next day, hand delivered. I also wrote my resignation letter effective immediately and I left town that night with my mother. My parents came to Delhi Air port to see me off. I did not think any of us realized it was my final departure from India for ever.

My first stop was at London Heathrow Air port. I was going to spend a few days with my friend Hema, whom I knew from my NCC training days. Since then she had married her sweetheart, Abbas, a Muslim. They had immigrated to the UK, where he was a school teacher, and she was a house wife. They had two kids. They were the happiest Hindu-Muslim couple that I knew. Abbas was a very nice person. I took them to a London Theater, and saw fiddler on the roof before I left for Texas.

After a short stop over at JFK to go through Customs, I landed in Texas, where my friend came to receive me. She looked more like a man than a woman because she was dressed in pants and a blouse with her hair cut quite short. She drove a big Buick car. Her house was beautiful and well decorated and she had a cute little dog. We talked, before she showed me to my room and the bath room, and then I retired for the night.

It was quite an experience for me, because I did not know what was ahead. After I got over my jet lag, and acquainted with my living conditions, I started to do things to help my friend in her house- hold chores like cooking, cleaning etc. I started writing to my friends in India and the U.S., including the Professor. I also mailed a letter to Canada to determine if the post doctoral fellowship offer was still valid.

I was getting used to Texas which was hot and humid and in the evening there was a concert by the crickets. Some thing was amiss about my friend. I had lived in a house with 10 girls and a house mother and her husband, but had never seen a person like this lady. She was a very opinionated, domineering Republican. She was curious about my single life, and she was aware of our custom to be married arranged by parents, and she wondered how I escaped that. She disliked Democrats with a passion. She told me about her life and that she did not like being a female, therefore she underwent a total hysterectomy, which I thought was odd.

Those were the Primary election days, and Bobby Kennedy, brother of slain President John Kennedy was gaining in the polls to be the Democratic candidate for the National election against the Republican candidate. My friend was furious, and said that she will leave the country and move to live in a tiny island called Tenerife in the Atlantic Ocean if Bobby Kennedy is elected. I did not quite see why she disliked

Democrats as I happened to like John Kennedy, besides I was not a U.S. citizen and not entitled to vote, thank God.

My friends started to get in touch with me soon after they got my letters. One of them was Linda who called me to say she was married now and living very close to where I was, and that she and her husband would like to come and take me out to dinner. I was very happy that I would see her soon. She was my dear friend from my University days. She was quite a bit younger than I was, but very street- smart. As decided, she and her husband, Richard came to pick me up. She was surprised to see me in a Dress and not in a Sari, I told her I am in the process of becoming an American. I introduced them to my friend but Linda did not hit it off with her and I could sense that. I met Richard for the first time and thought he was a cool guy. As we got in the car, to go to dinner Linda blurted out where did you find this person, she is a lesbian. I was stunned to hear that and I asked her how she knew; she said it was so obvious. I started thinking that some of her ways were not what I could relate to, and that could explain it for now. We talked about my stay, and I was determined to move on as quickly as possible. Well, I thanked Linda for helping me to see what was going on. This was another one of those lucky auspicious "muhurtams" (moments) that Linda happened to be in Texas at that time.

They dropped me off and said to keep in touch and left. My friend was waiting for me and she told me she did not like Linda and her provocative way of dressing. Linda was wearing a beautiful mini dress and her hair was very well done, at the time she was only a 23 years old. I answered her and said, I think her husband liked the way she dressed, so what does that matter if you do not like that. She of course, did not like what I said. After Linda's visit I sensed her behavior had changed, and she was quick to give different opinions from mine. That day was the California Primary election; the result would determine who will be the Democratic candidate for the general election. And Bobby Kennedy was going to be that candidate so my friend was very upset. Then the news broke that Robert Kennedy had been shot and fatally wounded. I called her at her work to pass on the miserable news; she was certainly not unhappy, as a matter of fact she sounded all right and said now I do not have to make arrangements to leave the country. I could not take it any more. I was getting used to the American way of candidate selection. Despite Linda's observation that my friend was a lesbian, I did not know what attracted her to me; did she think I was a closet lesbian and she would eventually help me out of the closet? I do not know. I had no opinion about her life style, but I sure did not belong there.

I also had heard from the Canadian University, and the Department head wrote that yes, the offer still stands. I was quite desperate to move from Texas and accepted the offer. My friend got very angry, but I told her it was very difficult to get a job in the U.S. or Texas in particular, because of the on going Viet Nam war, which was drying up funds for research, and that is what I was looking for. She had to accept my decision, though grudgingly. I left her place for good and moved to Canada. It was an experience I will never forget.

My Short Stay in Canada

I was happy to be in Canada and earn some money for a change. The people in the department were from all over the world including the UK, India and Pakistan. I liked the country; they are quite conscious of their big neighbor to the south, bordering on a complex. I was asked to help my boss's graduate student, a Pakistani. Who was a very nice person, I had never met a Pakistani before, and even though I knew they were like the Indians, they were mainly Muslims. Soon we became friends that generated plenty of rumors in the Pakistani student community. Canada has some of the most beautiful natural sceneries in the world, but winter is severe and harsh. I started feeling the cold from the month of October. Suddenly the weather changed. It started snowing and I had problems going about, because I did not have a car, and transportation was worse than in the U.S. Soon winter came in November; one has to keep the car plugged in, to a block heater, otherwise it will not start. I just did not want to go through the winter in Canada and I was lucky to see an advertisement in a scientific magazine about a fellowship at University of California, Los Angeles so I called to find out about the position. I was told to file an application with them, which I did and I got the fellowship. Soon after I announced my decision to leave Canada, and my friends kidded me for going to smogsville Los Angeles. At that time I would take any place to get out of cold Canada.

I stopped in Seattle, Washington on the way to LA. I was a house guest of my Jewish friends whom I met in India. He was a Professor at the University, and his wife Lillian was a house wife. Her mother, who lived with them, was a Polish Jew. After dinner, I was helping Lillian with the dishes, and I noticed my dishes were different and were put away separately. I asked her why my dishes were handled differently and she replied sheepishly, that it is the orthodox Jewish custom, that non- Jewish guest dishes have to be dealt with separately. I told her I was used to that sort of discrimination because in India that was very common in a Brahmin home, and likewise dishes are done separately. Well, I learnt some thing new.

My Life in Los Angeles

I moved on to Los Angeles, and thanked God for listening to my prayer and for bringing me back to LA within three years from my last visit on the way to India. Another friend, a Japanese lady, Dr. Aiko met my plane and took me to her apartment where I met her family; her husband Dr. Tetsuro, and their two daughters, Junko and Moriko.

They were visiting scholars at the University of California at two different departments. She worked in my department therefore, she came to receive me. She took me to my hotel before I moved to an apartment. She was a very smart, friendly person, and for Japanese she was tall and heavy set. I was very happy to meet such a good person. I had such a stereotypical opinion about Japanese women, and she was so different. She was a hard- working woman, who took care of her family while doing Medical research. She helped me find an efficiency apartment near UCLA, so that I could go about by local bus, the Blue line, I was not ready to buy a car yet. I reported to the Department next morning, a mini United Nations; there were Polish, Israeli, Dutch, Danish, Taiwanese, local Japanese, Japan Japanese and now an Indian. Our boss was an American Jew. My fellowship was financed by the U.S government, and I was supposed to receive a stipend of $1000.00 a month, within a few months the administration told me that they are readjusting my stipend to half, because the government had reduced the funds, as the Viet Nam war was still on. I stayed on in my efficiency apartment; there was no way I could splurge to move to a one bed room apartment on that revised stipend. I had to manage every thing on $500.00 a month and LA was expensive.

I was getting to know my work place where they published the UCLA news paper called" Bruins". One day at the coffee break I picked up the paper and was surprised to see that Ravi Shankar, the Indian musician (Sitarist) was going to be in town and giving one recital. I just murmured oh Robu mama (uncle) will be in town. This was considered as name dropping, which they thought was common amongst Indians. Those were the days when the *Sitar* was very popular with the hippie students, so was Ravi Shankar. One of my work- mates asked me if I was going to attend the program. I said no, because I was not much interested in music. This person took it for granted that I was name dropping, so she said that she wanted to attend and would I accompany her ? I knew she was challenging me, so I said yes I will go with you. We both went to attend the program and as Ravi Shankar appeared on the stage to a standing ovation, my friend asked me if I was going to see him. I asked her how she expects me to go through the crowd to see him but she did not give up, asking me again at the intermission and again when the program ended. This time I dared not say no, so we both proceeded back stage, and it was my good luck that RS was coming down the hall. I stepped forward and said *hello,* do you remember Shobhadi, (my mother)? Oh yes, are you her daughter? and he gave me a big hug. I introduced him to my friend, he noticed her accent and asked where was she from?

She said she was of Polish background. He told her that he was happy I came to visit him, because he would not have known me, as he had seen me as a little girl only, many years ago. Then he asked me about every body he could think of, and he asked a lady (she became his wife) to give me his telephone number, so I could get in touch with him. Of course I never did call him. Next day, at work word was around that I really did know him. RS used to live in the same neighborhood, and he was a regular visitor to our house. We called him uncle Robu. I do not remember when he left Varanasi but I did remember that he used to send picture postcards to us from far away places like Paris and London.

I was getting to know some people through the American Association of University Women or AAUW. I repeat again that the Americans are very good at organizing things, and this was an association of college graduates. Soon the Association invited me to a luncheon at their regional meeting. I was seated at the dais with a lady from San Bernardino, Olive, who had a Master's degree in Science, and she was a high School science teacher. Her degree was from UCLA; therefore we had some thing in common. We got along well and were friends for a long time. Olive and I took some out of town trips and the one I liked most was the trip to Mexico. Being such a dedicated mother she was terribly upset when her older daughter, married and in her thirties suddenly fell ill, I think it was a stroke that paralyzed her as she was in the hospital lying comatose. Olive felt her son –in- law was not doing enough and he was thinking of institutionalizing her. She did not like the idea, so she remodeled her house to accommodate the wheel chair-bound invalid daughter. That daughter, Melinda even recovered from many of her symptoms, so much so that Olive took her to Mexico with us, and we had a very good time together. I lost track of Olive for a few years, then later when I relocated in San Bernardino County, I tried to locate her, but without success. Finally, I mailed a short letter to her address, and there she was her name had changed; therefore I could not find her in the directory. She told me that she had married and while vacationing in Hawaii her husband passed away. This was her third marriage. Apparently she was not lucky in marriage. She retired from her teaching position and not long afterwards she passed away. I attended her funeral feeling very sad.

In one of those AAUW get together I met two ladies who became my good friends. One, Rita, was a rich single Jewish lady, very well traveled and educated and the other was a school teacher, Lillian. Lillian was very active with a literary society, another organization similar to a book club. She knew an Indian a single man, who was also a member. One day Lillian called me and said she wanted me to meet an Indian friend of hers. Every body wants to be a match- maker. I said yes, I want to meet him, so Lillian planned a dinner party at her Hollywood home, and got in touch with the Indian man, Keki. She wanted him to pick me up to go to her house for dinner to facilitate his getting to know me. To her surprise a lady answered Keki's phone, and she sounded as if she lived there. Lillian left a message to return her call, which he did, and he told Lillian that the lady who answered the phone was his wife. So there went Lillian's strategy of match- making. The Dinner went on as planned however, and Keki and his wife drove me. We became friends and they invited me to their home for parties, where I met many Indian Parsees (Zoroastrian), one of whom was a single lady and we became good friends.

Lillian was such a good person that I used to go to AAUW meetings just to meet her and some of my other friends. Unfortunately, Lillian and Rita both passed away unexpectedly.

I contacted the lady I met in the train on my way to the Grand Canyon when I was returning to India. She was pleasantly surprised to hear from me since I was calling from LA. One day she and her husband came and picked me up to spend the day with them. She had prepared a very good chicken dinner and they took me to their home. I did not visit them a lot because they lived far from where I lived, and I did not have a car; LA is a place where if you do not have a car you have very restricted mobility. One day she called me to give me the bad news that her husband died of colon cancer, and she was moving back east closer to her relatives.

At work I started my research but soon I learnt that the big grant that financed the whole department would be discontinued. The government did not want to finance such basic research consequently we will all get our pink slips. In view of this news I started looking into other avenues to branch out.

One day I had a call from an Indian who said he was the President of the International Student's Association. He invited me to join the association but I told him that because I was not a student any more I did not think I belonged there, but then I will be happy to meet him. I mentioned to him I did not have a car, so I would need a ride. I think I met him for the first time at the University Cafeteria, where I used to go for my lunch. He was quite an impressive young Indian man. Another time he called me and asked to me to join him to go to the Airport to receive an Indian girl coming to join the UCLA graduate school. I decided to go. He picked me up and we arrived at the airport on time to receive her. However, when she arrived, she walked away with some other people waiting for her. This girl later became my Indian friend's wife. I did not realize at the time that it was love at first sight, because I knew at the time he had a steady French- girl- friend. I was thinking that this was a repeat scenario to what I experienced as I came to do my graduate work a few years earlier. We became good friends and we have stayed that way. This friend, Om, told me a little bit about his background, and I was impressed how he came from a family that had very little education and meager financial means. He was born in rural Punjab just prior to the India/ Pakistan partition; therefore, he had heard about the blood shed that occurred near by when Hindus and Muslims fought each other. Unfortunately, his older brother was a gambler who had gambled away whatever earnings were generated from their commodity - agriculture business. At the time he was just a toddler, who cherished the interest to become an Engineer one day. His perseverance was helped by good luck and he was eventually admitted to Aligarh Muslim University where he earned his engineering degree, and then moved on to do his doctorate at UCLA. His meteoric rise to what he is today would make a book worth writing, so I hope that one day he sits down and does just that.

Om introduced me to his English friends, a couple with a daughter, Jennifer. One day I went to visit them and found they were the nicest people that I came to know. We are friends now for ever and I have spent many days with them. John and Daphne are very fond of Indian food, and she cooks the best lamb curry that I know off. They are now grand- parents of twins, a girl and a boy. Daphne and John were in India as "army brats" Daphne was born there in Nazirabad in Hyderabad, now Andhra Pradesh. She left India and returned to the UK when she was eight years old. That was during WW II , and she moved around from place to place in England and aspired to work for the United Nations in Geneva, but was not quite of age yet, therefore, she moved on to Vancouver, Canada to make her life there as a young girl barely age 20. John was born in the UK and his parents brought him to India as a little toddler, and he also moved around with his family from one army post to another. He was sent to Darjeeling for his education, and got his Senior Cambridge diploma there. Soon after he left India prior to India's independence from Britain. John and Daphne met each other in Nilgiri Hills, South India when they were kids, how romantic could that be. They met again in England and later in Canada and decided to tie the knot. He had been in the television industry most of his life after a short stay with the British army in Germany, where he learnt photography. He has a big circle of Indian friends and he loves visiting India and goes there often, but Daphne never been back to India to visit.

Om and his wife Indira moved to Texas after finishing their degrees, and they are settled there. Together they started an IT computer consulting company. The business flourished so much that they split it into two companies, and they both became chiefs. As a CEO, she excelled in sales and marketing. The high light during this time in her life as she told me was her visit to the White House during the Clinton administration, as an elected delegate from North Texas to attend a conference on small businesses. She was also interested in social activities and was elected to Dallas Forts Worth's minority business development, in which she served for three years. She is now actively helping in adult literacy, and served as the board president of the adult literacy organization in Texas for three years. She is also helping her husband in his literacy project for India called Pratham. Om and Indira are also proud parents of two daughters.

I still did not have a car, so I depended upon the Japanese and Polish friends in my department, who helped me very generously. I spent a lot of time at my Japanese friend's house; however, so far I met her husband only one time. She always told me that Tetsuro is busy doing his research to finish up before they return to Japan. They were to return soon, she leaving with the kids ahead of him by boat, and he leaving later by air.

Finally, a day arrived when we all were told that most of us who were financed by the grant will loose our jobs, so every one got busy looking for jobs elsewhere. I had applied for a special Fellowship, a govt. grant. The department was planning a farewell dinner to be held at the Polish lady's house where she and her husband had a very pretty house in the west side of Los Angeles. We got together there for cocktails followed by dinner, which was prepared by our helper who was a Kurd from

Kurdistan, a disputed part of Iraq at the time. I remember, he used to tell me that his passport was from India. He was very anti Iraq and used to voice his opinion for a separate state.

That day started with a bit of good news for me. My Special fellowship application was granted for two years by the National Institutes of Health so I was ecstatic. To celebrate, I had a cocktail. The evening was enjoyable but my cocktail was doctored deliberately to see its effect on me, so I was feeling very tipsy. At the dinner table I was seated across from our director, and suddenly I was looking at a big Pinocchio nose on his face, and I knew I was in trouble. I excused myself from the dinner table, as I felt sick. I spent the night at her place and left the next morning to go home.

That fellowship gave me some time to think about my next step. My Japanese friend was to leave soon, and she confided in me something that I was stunned to learn. To make the long story short, her husband was having an affair with a woman from an eastern block country which in those days there were East-West tensions. When she found out she was very upset. This other woman was also at UCLA in his department and after completing his work he was going to visit her country. My friend asked me for some suggestions. My suggestions were to try to stop his visa from that country, and buy some expensive diamonds to deplete their savings account so he would not lavish the lady with gifts. She liked my idea and we went shopping. She bought herself a very expensive diamond ring, and she went to that country's visa office, but had no help. She could not stop him from getting a visa. One day she came to my apartment and asked if she could use my telephone. She telephoned her father- in- law in Japan and talked for about an hour in Japanese, I did not understand a thing, but I could feel the tension in that conversation. She paid me about $90.00 for that telephone call. I was very sad for my friend. Her father- in- law told her not to make any noise, and to leave the USA quietly. She told me I could buy her car after her husband leaves the country. She was such a dear friend of mine, and I miss her.

One day after she left, her husband came to our department, told every one about his affair, and gave me the car key for about $200.00. Everybody was stunned and I told Tetsuro there was no need for him to talk about his affair and that; his wife did not talk about it. He ignored me which changed my opinion about Japanese men. Women there are still not at the same level as men. We kept in touch for quite some time before we lost touch. I am sure the girls are grown women, and grandmas themselves. Perhaps by now the situation has changed in Japan and women are enjoying better status in the society.

A friend of mine, Kamala was visiting me from India, and she told me that another friend whom I knew in India was also living in southern California. She gave me her telephone number and later I got in touch with her. Chitra was my colleague and taught mathematics. She was a very smart, petite pretty woman. She was not very happy with the boring life in Varanasi, and wanted a change so she went ahead and took her chances in the national competitive examination and was selected for Indian Foreign Service, which was quite an accomplishment. She soon left Varanasi, and after some training in Delhi she was posted to Vienna, Austria to the Indian Embassy. Some of my friends knew her family, and told me some news about her. This was that she was very lucky to meet a very handsome, intelligent Indian man, whom she met on the ship on the way to Vienna and they were married. I wondered why not the other way around that he was lucky to get a girl like her. I was happy to meet her and her family, after so many years. She and her husband studied at Stanford University, she earned a master's degree in Statics while her husband earned his PhD degree in Engineering.

They settled in southern California and when I met her she already had three children.

Meantime, in India, my youngest sister was married. I just could not have gone there because I had started my new fellowship, and I had to close down my work to leave the place. These were the drawbacks of staying abroad; you miss out on the important occasions at home sad or joyous. Soon my sister came to Germany, and I visited her there.

Since I was doing relatively better financially, I moved to a one bedroom apartment in the beach city of Santa Monica. I still did not have a car, because I had totaled the car that I bought from my Japanese friend. I did not have insurance on the car, and I had damaged the back yard wall of the neighbor's, and I had to go to Emergency to have my upper lip sewed up. The neighbor dropped by to complain about his damage and ask for repair money. Seeing my condition, when he learnt I did not have insurance, he left me alone. He was one of those very good Americans, and I learned the importance of car insurance. Since then I bought insurance as soon as I bought a car.

My move to Southern California coincided with my friend Linda's move with her husband to northern California where I used to visit her often by air. Those days flying there by PSA was $ 10.00 one way after 11 o'clock at night. As usual we discussed every possible topic. One time as I was getting ready to take my flight back, Linda suggested I read her husband's palm. Grudgingly, I agreed, and I told him that his hand indicated that he had two marriages and that he had two sons. He really was very uncomfortable with my readings and he said out loud I don't believe palm reading any way. We stopped and left for the air port. As I arrived back in my apartment, my phone was ringing, Linda was calling, and she said what I said about her husband was true because she was his second wife, and he does have another son from that marriage. It was news to me; I did not know his background.

A similar encounter happened with Barbara. She always insisted that I read her palm as she wanted to know if she was going to marry an elderly gentleman. She did marry the gentleman whom I had met in her school. He was the senior teacher in the department. He was a chain smoker and succumbed to lung cancer soon after their marriage. I stopped reading palms after that. Barbara then married a third time; this time she invited me to attend her wedding. I had met the gentleman earlier and often wondered why she wanted to marry him. He had no job; he did not drive, so he was sort of a parasite. I do not know what she liked in him to consider marriage. It was a small wedding attended by their families and me. The wedding took place in a small chapel in Alexandria, Virginia, and I was told that the first President, Mr. Washington, used to pray there, which was interesting to know. Barbara was quite an educated woman, she had obtained her Master's degree and for her thesis she had interviewed many celebrities including Mr. Reagan who at the time was ex governor of California between jobs preparing for the President's position.

Life in Santa Monica was very good. I used to visit the beaches, and the life was peaceful, compared to LA living. There at the beaches I met a young French Canadian nurse, Anita, who was very pretty and very sociable. She felt a kinship with me as commonwealth subjects. She lived in a nearby apartment and she used to give me rides, because I still did not have a car. I had had another car accident but that time it was not my fault, so the damage to my car was paid for. I was hesitant to buy a car and go on those freeways. But soon I got over my fear, and bought several cars over the years, all new and U.S. made, and freeway driving was a piece of cake.

My friend Anita was a very good cook who loved to arrange small dinner parties. Some of her friends also became my friends for life. One of them was Myrium from Columbia, S. America. She was very young and petite and came to the USA as a tourist where she met a German immigrant, fell in love and married him. Together, they made a good life and when I first met her she was pregnant with the first of two daughters. We have been friends for more than 35 years. After Anita's room mate Lucy got married and left, Anita started sharing her apartment with her new male friend, a quite handsome, German guy, who was younger than she, and had his own business. She soon left her nursing job and went to work at his business.

Before I leave my UCLA days account, I should share my unique but very sad account of the fellowship training. I was told that as a part of the training I have to attend some Grand-rounds, which was a once- a- week Doctor's gathering, where they presented their difficult patients for consultation and advice. These get togethers took place at a VA (Veterans Administration) hospital. I witnessed young male patients suffering from a disease that no one was familiar with. The guys had abnormal blistery looking lesions on various parts of their bodies, including their groin area. It was called Kaposi's sarcoma.

These patients's were emaciated gay men. At that time Scientists were zeroing in on the cause and defining the disease. It was in 1981 and shortly after I left UCLA the Scientists were the first to describe it as Acquired Immunodeficiency Syndrome or AIDS, a fatal disease caused by the HIV virus in male homosexuals. This is now pandemic all over the world. The virus is transmitted by body fluid exchange (blood or semen). The virus attacks white blood cells, thus the body looses its capacity to fight infections, and becomes the victim of secondary infections, called opportunistic infection. The end comes soon. This no longer is the disease of the homosexual men; it is a disease of the heterosexual population as well, as in India, which has the dubious distinction of being the number one in AIDS cases in the world. This disease can be managed by drugs, such as protease inhibitors (AZT), and need not be fatal.

I was attending a meeting in New York City and since I was going to be in NY, I had planned to go to India from there. I took a Pan Am flight, which was one of the last flights before Pan Am closed down for good. The flight was full of Indians with children, and lots of baggage. I thought I would have to travel like this for 14- 15 hours but then an American couple embarked who had seats next to me. We introduced ourselves and he said they were going to Katmandu, Nepal just to get away from it all. I asked him what he was talking about "get away from it all". He said quite a few of his friends had passed away within few months; therefore, he wanted to leave and go as far away as he could go. I said you sound as if there is an impending epidemic and he said yes they died of AIDS, and that he was a homosexual.

I felt scared, even though I was fully aware that the disease was not communicable just sitting in close proximity. Next morning I saw the poor guy's eyes which were red, and already infected. He said he had some eye medicine that was going to take care of it. His female companion was a smoker, so she stayed at the rear of the plane. This man was very handsome and a nice, friendly fellow, and was an artist in NY; I wonder what happened to him after we said good bye in Delhi, India.

My life beyond UCLA

Soon the two years were gone. My fellowship ended and I was looking for a job. I was an immigrant, thus restricted in the job market. Besides, I found subtle gender discrimination also in the job market. I started working at a Hospital in LA but soon that hospital had to be closed, because it was on an earthquake fault. Most of us working there dispersed to different hospitals in LA County, and I landed in Martin Luther King Jr. hospital in south central Los Angeles. To get there I had to drive a long way taking three or four freeways, so I was thinking of moving again as is the typical life style in California where people change their residence frequently. As I was mentioning this to the Professor, who was back at his University in the U.S, he mentioned that he would like to retire in southern California where he could live with me in a town close to the ocean. I took him up on his suggestion, and went scouting for an apartment in a beach city, closer to my work.

At the King hospital I came to know Black America up close and personal. This hospital was a new addition to the LA county hospital system. It was very much needed for that area, because people did not have any kind of medical assistance. The area was the famous ghetto called Watts, where violence was a common occurrence. My laboratory assistant was a young black woman, who was an excellent worker, but most of her time was spent finding out the latest news about the "brothers and sisters". She was a single woman in her thirties, and she was a mother of three kids, each one by a different father. The majority of the Doctors at the hospital were non-blacks and the other employees were mostly Blacks. Once I faced a problem hiring a research assistant. I wanted to hire somebody with some science background and administration advised me to advertise on bill boards and may be in a local newspaper. I did, but no one applied for the job, so I advertised in the prestigious science magazine called *Science*. I got good response and there were quite a few applicants to choose from. I interviewed most of them by telephone, and hired a man from Utah, who had some of the technical knowledge that I was looking for. When he joined the job, this blue eyed blond young man created a sensation by his presence. There was rumor going around that I was partial to the young man but my black assistant took care of that. She said "no black person came through that door for an interview", in other words no black candidate applied for the job. Any way, Bill the young guy from Utah was just as surprised to see all the Blacks as the Blacks were to see him working with them. They got along well, after the initial shock. Bill left after one year working there, and he kept in touch with me, I wrote several letters of reference for him.

I became a U.S. citizen, and witnessed the U.S Presidential election, this time I was voting, therefore, I went to listen to Jimmy Carter, a Democrat, and a little known governor from the southern state of Georgia who came to the hospital. The Democrats always stopped at the Black institutions for their votes. The majority of Blacks are Democrats. I voted for Carter, and as a first time voter I sure was glad he was elected.

Time was passing, and my friends kept telling me that I should have a physical examination, including mammography, about which I had been procrastinating. I finally decided to go ahead with it. The radiologist, a lady I knew, told me that my mammogram was not quite what it was supposed to be, and that I should consult a general surgeon. I talked to a lady Doctor, a friend of mine and she suggested a general surgeon in Beverley Hills. I made an appointment, and went to see him. He looked at the x-ray and suggested surgery. Those days, surgery meant total mastectomy. Well, I had to decide whether to go through with it or not. I was hospitalized for a breast biopsy, which was the hardest decision of my life. I had to sign papers that in the event the Dr. finds malignancy, he would remove my breasts. I was already in a hospital bed when the Nurse came to request my signature. I was hesitant so she said you can walk away if you do not want to sign. I told her to come back after a while. I had some weird sensation in my left leg, which was intense muscle twitching. I remember my mother was a believer in some of those signs, if this was on my right leg that meant bad news. Well I felt good, as if some super natural power told me to go ahead with the surgery, so I called the Nurse to sign the papers and my twitching was gone. In the morning I was wheeled into surgery room and when I woke up, and I felt that my left breast was still there, so I was ecstatic, but I was not in a regular recovery room, instead I was hung up with all sorts of tubes and electrodes stuck all over me. In the room there was another bed, with an old man with similar connections on him and he was dying. I realized I was in a Cardiac care unit.

My surgeon walked in and said you had a benign tumor, and that a quarter of the breast was taken out in the procedure. He continued, however, we almost lost you and that will be explained to you by the anesthesiologist. He told me that I had a bad reaction to the anesthetics used to put me to sleep; in the process I went hypotensive and almost lost my life. Both the doctors suggested that if I had to undergo any surgery again, I should let them know my sensitivity to such chemicals. This was my third visit to the doorstep to the other world.

Anita, my friend who tried to call the hospital to find out how every thing went, got news black out about my condition, but since she was a nurse, she knew how to go about finding out what was happening. That evening she came to visit me, and told me all about it. Those days they did not have the modern way of doing a needle biopsy followed by lumpectomy if needed, therefore, they removed a quarter of my breast while I remained under anesthesia and they sent tissue for a pathology work up. When I was released from the hospital I recovered at Anita's where she really took good care of me. I had telephoned my sister about my going to the hospital, and when she learnt from Anita about my predicament she hurried over from Germany to visit me. I liked that. I appreciated Anita's help and my sister's visit tremendously. This hospital visit was covered by my Health insurance, which I had through my job. Health insurance is very important and usually obtained through the employment. I wish an insurance system was available to Indian people in a big way, so that they could take care of themselves easily without draining their nest egg, I say this with a few reservations. In the USA health insurance is a speculative business, and there are many horror stories in the news about how the insurance companies prey on people's health. In my opinion health insurance should be better regulated and speculation removed.

I did move, and rented a very good apartment in the beach city called Redondo Beach, and Professor came to live with me. Earlier, he had written to me and we had talked about living together and sharing expenses, like a symbiotic set up. He liked my suggestion. He loved living by the ocean and for a change doing as little as possible. I was still driving long distance, and it was tiresome. Living by the ocean did not change my life much.

I was getting tired of driving and working there, and started looking for a change.

The King hospital was deteriorating and the latest news was that the Hospital was downsizing. Because it had myriads of problems in Administration and patient care, the county wanted to close it down, but it survived and was taken over by a different management. I am glad it has survived as that area urgently needs medical help. Fast forward, hospital is now closed at a great loss for that community.

The pharmaceutical company representatives always stopped by and gave all the news of the new medicines in the pipe-line, as well as news about other medical institutions. One of them told me about a new Veterans administration hospital recently started in the next county, and that they probably are still filling vacancies, so I acted on his information. That contact played a big part in my next move. Contacts, contacts and more contacts is the name of the game to find a job. I contacted the VA hospital for an appointment with their administrative chief, whom I happened to know from my UCLA days. He was always very friendly and kind to me so I went to see him and he invited me to lunch, which was nice.

I asked him if he had a vacancy for which I might apply, he looked at me and said that I was a little late, he had filled the vacancy already, but he suggested that I talk to the University medical center nearby. I arranged an interview with the gentleman he suggested that I meet.

I talked to my friend Anita about my changing jobs, and that I may have to move and she offered to drive me to the interview. I knew Anita was despondent, because her room mate, her boy friend, had moved out from her apartment which was quite unexpected because she was working for him at his store, and we were expecting them to marry.

He was a handsome German and younger than Anita. I knew him also, a nice friendly person. I always talked with him about my work and the various microbes that I worked with. Years later I met him at a German friend's home, and he reminded me about my scientific life that I had almost forgotten. I was amazed at all the detail of our talks that he remembered. He went out of Anita's life and met a nice German lady, whom he married soon after.

Going back to our trip to my interview, Anita looked happy and said she had good news to share with me. I was very happy to learn that she had met John, who was also a German, through our friends Roy and Myrium. My question was "is he older than you"? She said yes and I said good and I was happy that she went ahead and married him. I attended her wedding reception. John had an engineering background and was a very helpful individual. I remember one time as I was driving out of my garage and half way out, the heavy garage door broke and fell on top of my car, I did not know what to do so I called John for some ideas but instead he said he would come and help me. At the time they used to live about sixty miles away. Within an hour John was at my house, and helped me take the garage door off my car. This kind of help was not unusual for him. John and Anita now live on a ranch in a beautiful town called Temecula.

I met the gentleman who was the Chief of Infectious Diseases at the University medical center for my first of a few interviews. He was a very decent, friendly individual and a very religious man. This institution is built on a Christian religious foundation, and I was impressed by the place about which I had a very good feeling. I felt that I was in the Hilton Hotel lobby compared to MLK LA county General Hospital, which looked like a cheap motel. This was the first time I thought of working at a parochial institution and I must say it turned out to be a good move. Fast forward, years later people tell me that the place no longer is as good as it used to be, because it is practically working as a General Hospital, and it has deteriorated in general up- keep.

On my last interview visit the chief told me the "dos and don'ts" of the place. They used to observe strictly their religious underpinnings even at the work place. For instance, the chief told me that this place is strictly vegetarian; therefore, no non vegetarian food should be brought in. Of course, they did have an excellent vegetarian cafeteria, and I became hooked on their nutritionally correct vegetarian food. Furthermore, he also said that no one is allowed to wear jewelry but a diamond studded watch probably was acceptable. I remember the day I was driving to my job, and I thought I should not have diamonds in my ear, which I used to wear all the time. As I stopped the car to get some gas, I thought I should remove my diamonds. I was surprised to find that I had already lost one of my diamonds. I looked for it, but it was gone, and I was sorry because I did not have insurance and it was a loss of a few hundred dollars. It felt as if somebody was watching my diamond jewelry habit and took care of it.

This new job was about 100 miles from my beach city apartment, and freeways are the only way to travel. After a couple of days traveling 200 miles a day, I decided to move to an apartment in town for the week days and return to the beach city over the weekend. It worked all right for a few weeks, and then my beach city apartment, which was operated by a corporation, decided to sell those apartments as condominiums. They gave me the first preference as a buyer for about $200,000.00. Los Angeles and the nearby neighborhood properties had already appreciated beyond my reach to buy such properties, besides it was just an apartment, and I did not want to invest that much. Therefore, I decided to move inland. Properties were still available at a very reasonable price and I discussed my decision with my apartment mate, the Professor. He was quite unhappy about my move, because he did not like to live inland where the air was much polluted. The Professor used to be a chain smoker but even though he quit smoking several years ago, he was suffering from emphysema, a lung disease. Residing by the beach was good for him, but under the circumstances, financially, and otherwise, he did not want to move to smaller accommodation by himself, so he decided to return to the Midwest. I was sorry to see him go, because I wanted to help in his retired life.

I bought my first house, but I regretted that I could not share it with my family. The house was only about $60, 000.00; at the time, and I thought it was a good buy and it was doable for me, because I could take a loan to finance my purchase and make the mortgage payment. People were skeptical about a single woman obtaining a loan; this was the gender discrimination that existed, but I got my loan thanks to my parents, who gave me my name which sounded very much like a man's name. I moved to my new home, but did not do the rituals that Indians observe. I sent my new address to all my family and friends. My house was quite comfortable, and had three bed rooms and two baths. The house was climate controlled with air conditioning and heating.

My friend Linda who then lived in Northern California suggested that I get in touch with her friend, a Jewish lady who lived in a near by town. I was very happy to know her, and that started another long-lasting almost like a family, relationship. I shall talk about her later but while I was getting settled in my new house, I had a call from the Professor to say that he wished to return to California to avoid the severity of winter. I said he was most welcome to come, but I cautioned him about the polluted air in my town. He arrived, and I picked him up at the airport, which was about 20 miles away. He was happy to be back.

My new friend, Florence lived in a near-by town to me, and she invited me to her house for dinner. It was my first face- to- face meeting with her and her family. She gave me a little background about her friendship with Linda. Florence's husband was an engineer with a reputable, big firm. He and his family lived all over the world with his job, and she told me that they lived in India also for about three years in Ranikoot, Utter Pradesh. This was a Birla's project. Birla was one of the foremost industrialist's of India.

Ranikoot was not very far from Varanasi and at the time Florence was pregnant with her fourth child which was born at the hospital there. This was another episode for them to describe the unhygienic condition of the hospital where she said that she became infected and was violently sick. She was lucky and was successfully treated with antibiotics, by a good doctor. However, she could not believe how patient's families gathered around in the hospital compound, cooking and doing all sorts of chores. I knew what she was talking about because I lived very close to a hospital. We had something in common; her son and I were both born in Utter Pradesh, India.

Her husband's job took them to Brazil; there they met Linda and her husband Richard who happened to work for the same company. As Americans, they stayed together and did many things as friends. They enjoyed their lives in Brazil. From all the accounts I feel this is a good country to visit, but I never got around to going there. But I do not regret it.

Florence's home is almost like a museum, with various artifacts collected from all over the world including many collections from India. She is a very good cook and I had many dinners and lunches at her place including the Jewish- religious Seder dinners. To reciprocate her hospitality, I used to invite them for curry dinners. They loved my improvised *Samosas,* and once her husband asked me to make four dozens of them for a party he was giving. I did, and for that he promised a beautiful birthday party for me, which Florence did while he was away with his job. Their two sons, one born in India were also fond of my Indian food. Their son, the lawyer loved hot Indian pickles and whenever I brought those pickle bottles, he would open a bottle and finish it quickly. A similar bottle will last for months for me. I was invited to his second wedding but I had to decline because it was the same day that the Olympics opening ceremony in Los Angeles was taking place, and I had a ticket to attend it. It was a $200.00 ticket, a gift, and I did not want to let it go. I realized my friend and the family were unhappy with my decision, but I knew the Olympics were not going to come to LA again in my life time, and I am glad I made that decision. After the Olympics, I invited the newly weds to a very good Indian restaurant and we enjoyed the evening.

As the days went by Florence started having health problems and she had heart bypass surgery twice. I do not want to enumerate her various health problems and besides her health, she had some other rough times, but she always bounced back and I often wondered how she did. I think this is a Jewish trait, the way people move on after adverse situations and never look back, is almost "God's gift". In India we sit and mourn and blame fate or think it is God's will.

I spent many Thanks Giving holidays with them. She always used her best China and crystal on her dinner table and she made fantastic Turkey dinners with all the trimmings. At the dinners her sons and their families would also be there. The lawyer's two daughters were Florence's darlings and I love them too as my "nieces".

One day Florence called me, and sounded very sad. I thought perhaps some thing terrible had happened to her husband, because one always starts with the oldest member of the family. No it was not him, but one of her grand daughters had been murdered in a senseless act. When I asked her what happened, she told me that Tasha (the murdered girl) was sitting in her car at a fast food restaurant when a man approached her for her car. When she refused, he took out his gun and shot her. She then went to the telephone at the restaurant while bleeding profusely, called 911, and died shortly after. The guy took the car and drove off and to close the story, when the Police closed in on him he shot himself. I was stunned to hear that and felt numb. I went to Tasha's funeral; she looked so pretty lying there in the casket. She was cremated and apparently, she had had a premonition, and told her family that in the event death comes she should be cremated. Unfortunately, the family had a continuing streak of bad luck, because the second daughter was involved in a car accident, and is now paralyzed from the waist down. It was so sad when I saw her at the rehabilitation center. Her oldest son, who was a Viet Nam veteran, died of cancer. This is why I said earlier about Florence's will power to bounce back and resume the routine of life. I admire this quality very much.

I faced my first tragedy, and that was my father's passing. I had just started the new job and moved my residence from the beach. In India they send such information by telegram, and that is what they did. In the U.S. telegrams are almost a dying breed, and the telegraph office could not locate me by phone and I did not know what they did with the telegram. I came to learn the news by a letter which reported that every thing went off well at his funeral and so on.

I appreciated very much the way the people at my new job treated me. First they sent me a big food basket consisting of breads, apples, cheeses, cookies etc., and then when I started my work, a priest who used to visit, said a special prayer for my father. I could not believe how good these people were to me. They really helped my grieving.

The Professor kept busy doing the things that he liked to do, like tending the fruit trees, and making a vegetable garden in my backyard. There were peach and nectarine trees plus a grapevine, and with Professor's right touch, each tree was producing a lot of fruit. I gave away bags full of fruit to my neighbors and also canned some to put away.

I was involved in a big project; therefore I used to get home late, one day as I returned, the house looked dark, the drapes were not drawn and the mail was not picked up. The Professor usually took care of all that, so I started getting a sinking feeling and hoped he did not get any thing out of the ordinary. Well, he was not home. When he left to go shopping etc, he always left a note and took the local bus for transportation. According to the note he left, I understood that he departed quite sometime ago, and should have returned a long time ago. I just was very worried about him, and I decided I should stay put at home instead of going looking for him. I called one of my new friends to come and help me out of my situation. This man's wife, Hildah was the cashier at our hospital cafeteria, and a very popular Indian woman. Her husband, Raj was very friendly and he came immediately, by which time I had received some information about the Professor. The Hospital emergency called to talk to "the owner of the property" and said this gentleman was brought in as a "hit and run" casualty the result of a car accident as he was crossing the road. My first question was how is he doing and did he break any bones? They said it appears there is no bone fracture, but he had a concussion which he has just come out of, and he wanted me to visit him.

Raj, my friend and I visited the hospital Emergency room, and found the battered Professor. I could see he was happy to see me, and I was thinking how I am going to take care of him, when my friend whispered to me "he is not going to survive for long." He wanted to go home, and refused to stay in hospital. I took him home, though I knew full well the house was not suitable for his recuperation. It was mind over matter, and his *will* to survive brought him through, and he lived another ten years, but this was the beginning of a difficult decade to follow.

Gradually, he recovered from his traumatized state and felt well enough to travel back east. The insurance company of the hit- and-run driver settled the case with the Professor with some money, and he decided to return home and use the money to install a central air conditioner at his house. He was impressed by the central air conditioning in southern California.

Slowly, it was adjustment time for me; I had my own home, a piece of America. My friends and sister came to visit me, and I had good times visiting with them.

One day the Professor called to say that he was feeling very sick, and would like to return to California. From what he described to me it was clear that some disorder was evident in his gastro-intestinal system, with the result that he could not keep any food in his system. A few days later I went to the air port and picked him up. He looked very weak and emaciated. He could not eat any thing, and I started thinking that if I do not do any thing he will almost die of starvation. He had no medical help, because his physician was back east and I did not know where to take him, If I contacted a Doctor's office they would make an appointment for a month or two later and by then he probably would die. With all this in mind, I called my Chief. After he heard from me he contacted the Chief of Gastroenterology, and called me back within minutes to say take him to his clinic and he will see him right away. Professor grudgingly went with me to the doctor.

At the Doctor's office I stayed with him when the doctor examined him, because I knew he would be evasive and would want to go home.

The Doctor suggested that he should be admitted right away as he was dehydrated, and needed an intravenous immediately, but the Professor wanted to go home so I stepped in and told the doctor to please arrange for his admission to the hospital.

He stayed at the hospital for almost 10 days, and underwent a surgery. He had developed an esophageal ulcer because he had taken too many Aspirin tablets to take care of his aches and pains after the accident. He bounced back and Thanksgiving holiday was soon to follow, so I prepared a Turkey dinner for which his son and family joined us. That was the only time I had ever cooked a Thanksgiving dinner.

My secretary at the department told me that I should go and check out a house which was by a golf course and was for sale. I looked at the property, liked the location and I was thinking that it will be good for the Professor, because he always liked golf, and I thought it would help rejuvenate his failing health. The builder had built in the neighbor hood at the base of San Bernardino Mountains, and all the houses were sold except two. The Builder's agent gave me a price but I did not respond immediately. The agent called again and this time I accepted a reduced price, so I sold my first house and moved into the second house. When I was negotiating the price, the secretary was very surprised and she told me that in the USA one does not negotiate a price.

This move turned out well for the Professor, though he was no longer interested in golf. While he recovered from his GI tract problem, polluted air helped aggravate his emphysema. This is a disease that can not be helped much by modern medicine, therefore, he was getting very frustrated, and did not like his doctor's visits.

We took a vacation and visited his son and daughter- in- law in Tennessee. This was Bob's second marriage. We had a good time, but I could tell he was not quite comfortable and wanted to go home. I was quite stressed out as a care giver, and wanted to relax a little so that I would rejuvenate myself for the days ahead of me, and I decided to visit my mother in India, who was still alive. A friend of mine joined me on this trip and we decided to stop in Singapore for a couple of days.

Singapore, the one city country is a beautiful place to visit. I was very impressed with the fine floral displays especially, of all places, at the baggage carousel area of the airport. I had never seen such elaborate floral displays at a place where you impatiently wait to collect bags after a long flight. Anyway that set the tone for me and my friend for a two day stay in Singapore. We checked into a hotel and went sight seeing. We were very impressed with the city's cleanliness, and the beautiful landscape of the city, pretty looking flowering trees that looked perfect, to the point that they almost looked artificial. The city boasts about its cleanliness, and rightly so. We were also impressed by its cosmopolitan look.

After our visit we left this aesthetically pleasing city for Delhi, India. After the spacious well lit Singapore airport, Delhi looked drab and like a military camp with stern looking men at the immigration desks. There were a few poorly maintained potted plants here and there in unattractive planters. What a difference a few thousand miles made.

The Customs went off easily, but out side the airport it was a different matter altogether. This passenger- unfriendly airport is really a very bad place to visit. As one exits the airport it becomes obvious that this place never paid attention to building a meaningful parking structure for private cars, taxis or tourist vans. One has to walk about two kilometers to a taxi at the parking place, which was small for a big city like Delhi.

I wondered, as I traveled many times in and out of Delhi and paid departure taxes, how that money is utilized. Does this also go into the pockets of the airport authorities, as the saying goes "money just disappears in India, there is no accountability". In the city we saw cows roaming around unsupervised picking over the heaps of garbage which were all around. We read in the Western news reports that a cow walking on the railway line caused an accident and many human lives were lost in the process. But I, as a Hindu, could never understand how the sacred cow is so poorly taken care of. Perhaps Indians do not envision that the *mad cow disease,* that struck English cows, may also strike cows in India. The cows are eating all sorts of garbage and picking up all kinds of etiologic agents. In addition to cows, I found dead dogs on the roads.

We went sight seeing in Delhi, and visited the National Archives. It is an impressive building, and should be housing national treasures. Instead what I saw was very unpleasant. Rooms that were being renovated did not have protective coverings to save priceless articles from being ruined. There were empty cases in some rooms from which precious articles had been removed. Perhaps, some insider has already sold those to some foreigner for a good sum, who knows.

We also went to visit the Taj Mahal in Agra. It is the biggest tourist attraction in India, yet no attention is paid to spruce up the city. It is also not a very clean city.

I would like to suggest that the city administrators in India make efforts to clean up their cities, tackling this as a big undertaking almost on a war footing.

I finally got to my home town where my mother lived, and had a good visit with her. I was sad to leave her, but I knew she would prefer living in her own home.

When I returned back to the U.S, the Professor had been well taken care of in my absence. A Philipina woman who worked with me as a technologist, left her job to study for her MD degree overseas, which she did, and she was preparing for the U.S. medical board examination.

I let her stay at my house and study, because her place was not conducive for her to settle down and study, and in return I requested her to look after the Professor. She accepted my suggestion happily. She earned her MD at age 50, which was remarkable, but it was hard for her to get through the Board exams, therefore, she never became a licensed doctor. She almost faced financial ruin because of her MD endeavors.

Pets in my life

One evening as I sat in my family room watching a detective television program, I heard a noise coming from the adjacent kitchen. First, I thought it was the background noise of the program, so I muted the volume; it still persisted, I then got up and tried to look in the kitchen area, where I noticed a silhouette, through the glass window, as if a man was working with a tool to pry open the window to enter the house. My first reaction was to scream, shouting who are you? The man then escaped. I called the 911 number and was connected to the emergency police. The person answered that somebody will be there shortly. I was terrified, and waited for the police to come. No body came, so I called again, this time I was told "we are busy handling fatalities, and you are ok, so in time we will be there". I then called my neighbors, the young secretary and her husband. The husband, Butch came immediately with a big flash light in hand. I met him at the door and showed him where the man was working to gain entry. He looked around out doors and saw big foot prints on the dirt. His suggestion was to stay alert, and keep the out side lights on, and to call him in case it happens again, and then he left. Police did come later in the evening, and looked around, and gave me the same suggestion that Butch did, and left. All that time the Professor was in bed unaware what went on. I could not close my eyes and go to sleep that night.

Next morning at work I told my assistant that I wanted a dog. She said I do not know where to find a dog for you, but after lunch she returned and told me that "yes, there is a dog, and you can have a dog." I was very pleasantly surprised and happy to learn that I can have a dog. That dog belonged to her sister, but she did not want the dog any more. That evening I brought the dog home, and named him Lucky, because I saved him from going to the Pound. The Professor was rather irritated to see the dog, and said I could not keep the dog in the house. He said either the dog stays or he does. I said the dog stays, because last evening when some one was trying to break in, the dog would have saved me from the robber. The Professor calmed down and did not make any more comments, while the dog got used to living in the house. The Professor had a dog once in his life therefore, slowly he got very close to the dog. The dog behaved as if he was the Master, and responded to his commands, and the dog alerted him if his telephone rang in his bed room, by going back and forth between the family room and his bed room. He even walked the dog.

In addition to the dog, I also had the house electronically secured. It was a good bad or an ugly proposition to protect the house that way. Good, because I could sleep soundly at night with the alarm on, bad because I had to spend a fortune to install the equipment which those days was expensive, and had to pay a monthly fee to get the house monitored. And finally, ugly because when the alarm was activated the neighborhood was bothered by its loud noise. On one occasion when I was gone for a few days, and my second dog, Tim Tim was there at home, he was taken care of by my neighbor Barbara's daughter, Marlo and also my friend Molly. In the morning Marlo would come and release the alarm, and take care of Timmy in the morning, and then leave the house unalarmed for Molly to enter later. She was not given the alarm code, because she was an eighty year old woman and would have forgotten the code any way. That day Marlo forgot to visit the house, but Molly did come around noon to feed banana to

Timmy. When she opened the door, the alarm went off, and she did not know what to do, soon the police arrived and were about to hand cuff her and take her away to the police station, when they heard she came there to feed a banana to the dog inside the house. They told her "we have heard that kind of alibi before". While all this was going on the alarm company checked my reference list, and Marlo's mother who happened to be on my priority list, answered the call and told the company that Molly was telling the truth, and she is legitimate and that she visits there daily. That information was relayed to the police at my door, and Molly was set free. She fed my dog banana, and locked the door and left. On my return, I heard that story about Molly's feeding banana to doggie and almost being taken to prison.

This is how pets came in my life in the U.S., after Lucky, came three weeks old Tim Tim, this one was my dog, and I will write about him later.

My Neighbors

I lived mostly in apartments in southern California, and I worked all the time, therefore I had little opportunity to meet neighbors. Besides, apartment dwellers usually always keep to themselves, no body knows who lives in the next apartment. It is different in neighborhoods of single family homes. Before I write about this neighborhood I should write about my previous, neighborhood where I had my first house. An old couple lived in the next house to me; the man was in his nineties and his wife Genevieve was in her eighties. They were two able bodied old people that I came to like very much as neighbors.

He was a World War1 veteran. They lived there because of the Veterans Hospital which was nearby. In the U.S. veterans are well taken care of in the Veterans Hospital of the Federal government, for no charge. In this day and age this is a good deal, and the veterans deserve it. Genevieve did not drive, so her husband did all the driving. Occasionally, when he needed some work done at the hospital, he would ask me to drive him. Genevieve was like a mother figure to me and she was also curious about the Professor. One time I went to attend a professional meeting in far away Boston. Prior to my departure, I did grocery shopping for him and as he requested, I bought him a bottle of Vodka, hoping he would use it responsibly. While away I always called him from the hotel, but that evening he was not answering the phone and I was concerned. Genevieve had a key to my house, so I called her to enquire about the Professor. She discovered him in the bath room not in very good shape and she called 911. He was taken to emergency, where he was declared fine except that he had had too much vodka. Upon my return, I threw away the bottle and never bought another one. Another time, no body was in my house, and I had forgotten to shut off the air conditioner so on the way to the Airport I called Genevieve and she went in and shut it off. They were very good neighbors. When I bought my second property and moved on, she felt very sad to see me leave.

In the second house, as usual there was no time to socialize or get to know my neighbors. On my right side was a Black family who were friendly, but who kept to themselves except for the occasional *hi*. On the left side there were white families whom I knew too. One day at work I was paged and when I answered the page it was a Police officer on the line. He told me that the Professor had locked himself out of the house, and was at a neighbor's house. I left my work immediately and went to the neighbor's house where I met the Professor along with the two ladies, mother and daughter. I understood that the Professor forgot to take his key with him and a door that accidentally closed on him. Any way, I thanked the ladies for their help, and introduced my self. This was the beginning of my friendship with that neighbor. She was Barbara a young pretty woman, very much a New Yorker, who had moved there recently with her husband Mark and her only daughter, Marlo from a previous marriage. She also had a son, who lived with the father in Las Vegas. Barbara's mother, Mary was visiting her at the time. She was working at the local State University and her husband was in the Insurance business, and still is. Barbara and her family were my excellent neighbors and friends who helped me a lot, and I tried to reciprocate in whatever way I could. I remember one day Barbara, Marlo and I were taking a lunch break from a whole day of shopping. At the restaurant Marlo was telling her mother that she wanted to drop out of school, because she did not like some of the courses and she was not getting good grades. I started thinking about it and decided to help her with her school work. I suggested that to Barbara and they accepted it. At the time she perhaps was a junior in High school and she started coming to my house every evening and I helped her with her studies. This went on for a while and she started feeling comfortable with her studies and she improved her grades. She not only finished her High school but she also obtained her bachelor's degree, and we are proud of her. However, I did not get to really know Barbara and the family until after the Professor's passing, which happened soon after.

Now I like to introduce my friend Ingrid, the Doctor. She is an internist whose specialty is Infectious diseases, and she is a very good physician. In addition she is a beautiful person inside and out and also very tall. I recommended her to the Professor. He liked her very much because he felt she cared for him. He was quite critical of Doctors, because he thought they do not care for seniors.

Ingrid is Swedish American whose father was also a physician and a devout Adventist Christian involved very much in mission work. He supported many evangelistic projects financially mostly by radio. He left a charitable trust which is now administered by Ingrid, her sister and brother-in-law, to support various projects in Africa, Asia, Europe and the South Pacific. After finishing her M.D. degree in 1981 she went off to India on a mission elective, training as part of her residency program to a mission hospital in Ottapalam, Kerala for three months. There she met another Adventist physician, Mary, who was helping run a fertility clinic for infertile women. She thought "what irony, a country with a billion populations wants a fertility clinic". She understood that the infertile women are mistreated by their families in India.

She formed a very poor opinion of Mumbai, then called Bombay when she first landed in India on her way to Kerala. She was appalled

141

to see the poverty in shanty towns along the way from the airport to her hotel. She could not believe how India's financial Capital projects such a shabby poverty stricken unhygienic look, with piles of fecal heaps dotting the main road leaving the airport. She was of the opinion that no one taught them to dig a latrine to take care of their needs, and she felt disgusted when she arrived at the opulent hotel, and saw the contrast between the haves and have-nots. She stayed in Bombay for two days, and was anxious to move on. At the hospital in Kerala she delivered babies, treated ulcers, and anemia due to various parasitic infections. She says if she goes to India again, she will bypass Mumbai, or leave the airport by another route without going through the city of Mumbai.

Ingrid was a big help when the Professor passed away. She was the one who wrote the medical certificate of his death. I found the Professor lifeless in his bed one morning. Every morning, prior to leaving for my job, I prepared his breakfast, and he would come out, but that morning there was no sign of him, so I decided to go and look for him. I found him lying there cold. My first instinct was to dial 911 right away, which I did. The operator started asking many questions which I had to answer, so there was no time to think of my next step or to take a little time to comprehend what was ahead. Of course, this was no time for me to grieve either. Soon a police officer was at my door and he took charge of the situation. He was trying to figure out the cause of death. He asked me about his medications and counted all the pills, including his sleep medication. Once satisfied, he called his office to say the "gentleman died in his sleep, and that his house-keeper found him". By this time I was crying, but I had to compose myself to correct the officer to let him know, that the gentleman was living in my house, and that I was the owner of the property and I was no house-keeper. He noted down that information and shortly after, Professor was taken away by an ambulance.

Every thing was moving so fast that I did not have time to sit and mourn the end of a long relationship. I called his son, who lived in Tennessee, and he arrived that evening. He was such a big help to me that week that I cannot adequately express my appreciation. He took care of all the pertinent telephone calls relative to the Professor and I also took a few days off from my work. My friend Anita came shortly afterwards in the morning and just being there was very helpful to me. I appreciated that very much. I did not make a formal announcement of his passing, but whoever learnt the news sent flowers. I filled up his room with all the floral arrangements. Even though he was not a Church going Christian, I left a Bible, a Bhagwat Gita, and I lit a candle. As per his wish, he was cremated.

That week started out very well, it was my birthday, and to my utter surprise the Professor said "let me take you out to dinner". I said surely we will go out to dinner, and I made reservation in a swanky restaurant. He liked the place and enjoyed a good steak dinner. Two days after the dinner he was gone. I did not anticipate the way it played out. My sister came with her family and stayed with me for a few days. With the help of my friends and my family I recovered from my depression.

Soon after his passing, I lost my dog, Lucky too. The animals have a way to mourn also, the dog would sit at the door of the Professor's room which I kept shut, and refused to eat. He started limping so I took him to the Veterinarian, who operated on his leg, and that was the end of the dog. My sister and Anita insisted that I get another dog. One day Anita called me to say that I should at least take a look at the few remaining puppies at her neighbor's. I drove to her place one morning and looked at those puppies, and I fell in love instantly with two of them and brought them home. I named them TimTim and

DimDim, because one was smarter than the other. They were growing up so fast that I found it difficult to handle both of them, so when my Housekeeper asked me for one of them, I gave her Dim Dim. After a few days I went and checked to see how my doggie was treated, which was not very well; after that I did not look back.

Tim Tim, Timmy or doggie as I called him stayed with me for about 14 years before I had to have him put to sleep, which was very depressing for me.

I did not see my neighbor, Barbara after my first meeting with her, when I went to pick up the Professor, who was waiting at her place. Later one day she asked me where the Professor was. Because she did not see him taking his usual walks. I then told her of his passing. She felt bad and since then I got to know her well. Her husband, Mark, who is a very handsome tall guy, helped me handle my first doggie, Lucky, when he became incapacitated. It was very kind of him.

My Japanese girls

Barbara, who worked at the local University, suggested to me that I take a Japanese girl as a paying guest, that way I will have some company. I thought it was a good idea. There were a lot of them coming to her institution to learn English for three months, and they were housed with the local families. My first Japanese girl, Akemi was a very pretty young woman. Barbara drove her every day to her class, which was a big help to me. After her, I had three other girls, and I got to know Japanese girls up close and personal, and I formed certain opinions about them, but that does not justify a blanket statement about Japanese women.

Akemi was a vegetarian, but she ate fish, and I had no problems about her food. She hardly ate any meals but I had to keep a good supply of Oreo cookies and milk. Once in a while, I treated her at a Japanese restaurant although personally, I am not very fond of Sushi and stuff. She had a lot of male admirers, and she dated two or three at a time. Sometimes, I had a hard time determining who is coming and who is going. She used to wear heavy make up, such that her bath room sink stopped up and I had to call a plumber to take care of that. She was very easy to get along with, and often we visited in my family room, and sometimes watched television together. At the time President H.W. Bush's Gulf war was going on and every action was played out in front of us, she was so surprised to see American Women in the war zone. From my various visits with her, I felt she knew very little about the World. In one of her quiz questions she did not know who were the two European countries along with Japan who were defeated in World War II, but she learnt fast. I almost became her Mentor. One day, she told me that one of the white guys she was dating seriously wanted to marry her, and that he had introduced her to his mother. I sat her down, and asked her if she knew how much he earns? She said he will take a Sheriff's job, to which I said a sheriff does not make enough to support her life style; furthermore, she was not ready yet in the USA to supplement him financially. I did not mean to stop her from getting married, but she stopped dating the man and moved on. After she finished her three months course, she left for San Francisco, where she married a Sushi chef. He was an American citizen, and thus she obtained her immigrant status, and later divorced him. We are in touch and she is doing well financially. She is still single and she lives a colorful life.

After Akemi, I took two girls together, so that they would have company. I think that was a mistake. These girls came from well to do families, and they were not capable of doing any thing. One day they were going to cook the dinner and whatever they were going to cook was available in my kitchen. They wanted to make Macaroni and cheese and humburger. They were following the directions on the Macaroni box. It took them two hours to figure them out, and to decide what a saucepan was. After a good three to four hours they finished cooking the M-cheese and hamburger, which should have taken only 30 minutes.

My third girl was a mature young lady from Okinawa, Japan. She was an excellent housekeeper and helped me a lot. She was dating an African American GI, who was based in Hawaii, but she met him in Okinawa. She told me her mother did not like her relationship, and this had strained their relationship. I was going on an overseas trip, and I let her stay in my house while I was gone, because that way my doggie, Tim Tim would be taken care off at home in stead of boarding him in a kennel. One day she told me that her boy friend will be visiting her during my absence, and would it be all right if he stays in my house and drives one of my two cars, I said it was ok. Florence's husband Mac told me not to be foolish and not to let her boy friend stay in my house and drive the car. I had to reverse my position so I sat her down, and told her that I have been thinking about her boy friend's stay. I asked her what would her mother do. She said she would not have allowed him to stay in her absence. I told her that I agreed with her mother and have changed my mind, and he could not stay at my place. I suggested that he get a room at the nearby motel.

She got along with Tim Tim very well. One day as we returned from grocery shopping and she was helping me carry the bags inside, she returned after the first trip with a very worried face. I wondered what was going on. I got the impression that Tim Tim did some thing very bad, perhaps soiled the carpet. When I got inside, I saw first- hand what was going on. He had ripped open a big floor pillow with the result that all the cottony material covered the living and family rooms making a big mess. She helped me clean the rooms.

For a change, I really missed this girl. She left for Hawaii and after that I lost contact with her. Perhaps she married the American and lived happily ever after, I do not know. After her another girl came, and I do not remember her much. After these five girls, I decided not to have any more, besides the University also discontinued the program. I got the impression that they were rather juvenile, with very little knowledge of the World beyond Japan and the USA. They were quite fashionable, but I felt they lacked the curiosity to know about their female counterparts in the USA, or any where else, they only wanted to know American men. This was my limited opinion formed by knowing these five girls. I did have a very good opinion about my Japanese Doctor friend, but not her husband.

Mother & Daughter

I met Molly and her daughter Frances at Barbara's. They lived not too far from our neighborhood, on the other side of the mountain but easily reachable. They were of Italian background. Molly was a feisty little female nearing eighty and her daughter was in her thirties. At the time Molly's husband Barney was alive, but ailing and in his nineties. They had a dog named Six pence. Molly took good care of Barney and he finally passed away. He was a WWI Veteran; therefore, he was buried in a national cemetery. His passing gave Molly the freedom she always longed for. Her first order of business was to renovate the house including the kitchen. I saw two different personalities in Molly, one was a sweet old, motherly female and the other was a very demanding mother. She loved dogs very much, and after her dog was put to sleep, she became very close with my dog, Timmy. As I wrote earlier, she was almost taken to jail, because she came to feed banana to my dog. After her dog was put away, she found a lost dog and took him to the local animal shelter; she waited for a few days and then wanted to get the dog. She called me to help her get the dog, and suggested that I go there as the owner of the dog. I got the dog out and brought it to her, she named him Winchel. The dog is still with Frances in Oregon.

Molly was a very good Italian cook; I learnt my Italian cooking from her. She invited us often to her place for dinners. She had her own car; therefore she drove around herself to take care of her chores. However, she was very demanding, and wanted her daughter to cater to her demands. For instance, Frances had to take her cruising in the Caribbean for her vacation. Frances arranged every thing in her life to fit with her mother's demands. It never bothered her that her daughter did not go out on a date; because she was busy taking care of her mother. She had some health problems, and underwent bypass surgery, but her strong will power kept her going. She had recovered and took care of herself well. In one of her own self examinations she felt a lump in her breast. She quickly had a lumpectomy and underwent radiation therapy. I liked her very much for her spirited out look in life; however, I felt she was a bit selfish in her deals with her daughter. She was very kind to me and Barbara. One day she called me asking if I knew where Barbara's daughter Marlo was. I said I did not know. She was worried that her daughter, who was in the house alone, had met with foul play and she wanted to investigate. She and Frances came to my house and we went to Barbara's; there Frances pried open Marlo's bedroom window and went inside her house but did not find Marlo. The reason Marlo was not there was because her father had come from Las Vegas and taken her out to lunch. We felt quite foolish after that. Molly and Frances always helped me with the handy work around the house and saved a lot of my money. We celebrated Christmas and Easter holidays together.

Frances, was a young woman, and a very good individual, she worked in an office nearby and was a very good and popular employee. I knew Molly never encouraged her to have any male friend, because she believed her good life would be gone if her daughter got into a relationship. The house across from theirs was bought by a young man, who became interested in Frances, and invited her a few times to go bowling. Molly always went with them to the bowling alley. Sometimes, I asked her why she went with them. She ignored my asking or said why not. She was also of the opinion that the guy liked her just as much as he liked Frances.

I think Molly started worrying about me and Barbara influencing her daughter, and she started planning her move. Her alibi was that the local air was highly polluted and making her sick, which was true, therefore, they should relocate to a city or a state with much less air pollution. Frances and Molly drove about 1500 miles roundtrip to scout around a new state and a new town. It was their vacation trip. They returned, and announced that they were going to leave and live in Oregon which they did soon after and I missed them very much. They did visit us for Thanksgiving and at the time I also moved out of that neighborhood and bought a smaller house to down size my living. This house was in a gated community for active adults, where residents have to be at least 55 years old. I liked the living arrangement because of its security feature.

Molly and Frances visited me in my new place, and we enjoyed a dinner together.

They returned home after their visit and soon after Molly passed away. Up until the end she was driving herself to the Doctor and so on and I think she was about 85 years old. The end came rather quickly and Barbara and I traveled to Oregon to attend her funeral. As I saw her in that casket, I broke down and cried. I loved Molly dearly, and felt that I had lost a dear friend or relative. I was seeing the difference between her my grandma and mother, who just waited to die in the last years of their lives while Molly was fighting to stay alive and enjoy her life. Frances carried on well through all this. We did meet her boy friend, who worked with her at the same company. She married Michael and is enjoying her life in Oregon. We attended her wedding, and had a very enjoyable time. Barbara, Mark and I represented Frances's family at the church wedding. I am in touch with Frances by telephone all the time.

My retired life

I moved out of the neighborhood because I was about to retire, and there was no need to keep a big house, so I wanted to down- size my living and also, I was looking for security. But I did miss Barbara and her family. My friend Anita told me about a secured neighborhood, and suggested that I check it out and I did, and decided to buy one of those houses. It was a gated community for people 55 years or older. When I moved there, I was still driving to my work to finish the last few days; it was about 80 miles round trip for me. One day I was stopped by the highway patrol woman, and she cited me for two traffic violations. According to her, first I was tail- gating her and the second I did not have my new address on my Driver's license. I knew I should fight that ticket, because I was not following her very close, and I had already reported my change of address to the Department of motor Vehicles, and I was waiting for their revised driver's license. So, I went to court to fight the ticket and I was lucky; the highway patrol lady did not show up at the hearing. I had already stated my case and since she was not there the case was dismissed by the judge, and my driving record remained ok. These driving citations are not very good to have on ones driving record. The car insurance increases with these citations, therefore, I always took care of them as quickly as I could. I got perhaps 5-6 such citations over the years. I went to such traffic courts whenever I felt the citation was challengeable, and I won a few times but I lost a few times also.

Once, I also took my income tax case to the IRS (Internal revenue service) court. I always believed that if I am not doing something wrong then I should not be penalized. We in the U.S. observe 15th of April as a very important date. This is the last day to file an income tax report for the previous year, in which one can claim the overpaid tax amount, or pay the balance to the IRS if under paid. That year I had already filed my tax report and paid what ever I was to pay. My tax report was prepared by my Accountant. Then I received a letter from the IRS asking me to pay quite a few thousand dollars. That letter almost gave me a heart attack. According to the letter I had taken out a retirement account without reporting to IRS. My Accountant said you go ahead and pay it to keep IRS off my back. I did not agree with him, and started enquiring to determine where the mistake was. When I tallied my retirement accounts I found I moved one of my accounts from one bank to another, because the other bank was paying a better interest rate. Since it was a lateral transfer, and I was not taking any money out, I did not have to report to the IRS. So I went to the previous bank and asked them to show me if they had reported to IRS that I had cashed in that account instead of a roll over transfer to another bank. And there was the mistake. The lady did not check the box to say it was a transfer only and not cashing in and it was reported to the IRS. She was very apologetic about the mistake, and said she will write a letter accepting the mistake. With that letter in hand I called the IRS trouble shooting office; there is such an office with an eight hundred number. I felt the IRS was not that fearsome as we were made to believe. Again, I repeat, every thing is so organized. I talked with a lady who told me I could go to the IRS court to contest the letter; otherwise it will be hard to get rid of since every thing is computerized, and computers generate the same letter repeatedly. Luckily, I did not have to travel very far because they were bringing the court to the next town, otherwise I had to choose between Los Angeles and San Diego. At the time given to me, I went to Riverside, the temporary court site. I entered a big board room where a few people were sitting. I tried to state my case. I gave them my bank books with the dollar amount that was transferred from one to another bank; it was the same amount that I was penalized for. Then I produced the bank letter stating that it was a clerical mistake. After seeing all that they called the banks to verify what I had said. The case was then dismissed, and I was told to ignore the letter, and I would get that in writing shortly. I was elated beyond imagination. I did call my Accountant to tell him my story.

Timmy and I were enjoying our new place; we took long walks within the community. Some of the neighbors became good friends, but some were not very friendly. One friendly person I like to write about is Railynn. She was a single Anglo- American woman in my neighborhood and she had a dog. I met her at a Single's dinner, Ray and I sat at the same table and got acquainted. She was a retired High school English teacher and I found her to be a very knowledgeable and erudite individual. We compared notes about our traveling to distant lands, and she said she would be traveling to Thailand soon. She was almost running out of countries to visit. I noticed her hands were shaking, and she told me that she has the beginning stages of Parkinson's disease. She and I had similar political opinion which was a respite, because that neighborhood was as conservative as it gets. Even though I am a registered Independent and she was a registered Republican, I was considered a Liberal, belonging to the other party. Ray was a feisty strong woman, who took up causes to disseminate via the internet. Then her Parkinson's' became more serious, and she was knocking on every door seeking treatment. She underwent Deep brain surgery but though it did not help her a lot she did not loose hope, and kept working on the internet and made a net work of Parkinson patients. Then came the second Bush administration that vetoed a bill to finance fetal research. It was her cause to help to pass a veto- proof bill, which is yet to come. We both moved from that neighborhood, but we are in touch through the internet. She has lost her voice and therefore, we don't talk on the telephone. She is very active trying to move her cause forward. Last year as I was getting ready to visit India, I started to collect donations for an orphanage. She sent me, and without any questions, a $100 check. She still lives at her new place, but I do not know if she still drives or not. I wish and hope a new breakthrough in Parkinson's research comes soon to treat these kinds of diseases, and that she, along with a lot of other people have help.

Another person I would like to write about is Minka, who was a stunning looking woman in her late seventies. She was also at the same table as Ray, but two people away, so she sent me a message written on her paper napkin asking "are you on internet?" I wrote my internet address and sent it back to her. Sure enough, she sent me an e-mail when she returned home, and we became friends. She was an Interior-Decorator, and decorated many celebraty homes, including President Ronald and Nancy Regan. She was also an artist and worked with oil painting. One day she asked me to show her my picture when I used to wear an Indian sari. She borrowed my picture and made an oil painting of it. She gave that painting to me on my next birth day, which I appreciated very much; that painting hangs in my bed room. To celebrate her 80th birth day we went to Las Vegas, the gambling capital of the world. She enjoyed gambling very much. She also moved out of that neighborhood, to be close to her only son. We communicated by e-mail for sometime, but I do not know how she is now. She also lost her hearing; therefore I am not in touch by phone. One of these days I will make an attempt to find out how she is.

On my street I met some more neighbors; there were two racially – mixed couples. These were two older white men with relatively younger Japanese wives. I happened to have dinner with one of those couples, and at the dinner, I asked the lady where she met the gentleman. Her answer was in the USA, and she was a bank employee, where he was a client. She was a married woman, but her children were grown up and away from the family. She just moved out of her married life, divorced her Japanese husband and moved in with the white man, who later suffered a massive heart attack but survived. She then told him how she was barred from visiting him in the hospital by the hospital employees, because she was not related to him. She told him to marry her other wise she would leave him, and then they were married. I thought what a story I am glad I never faced such a problem.

There were a few single, widowed ladies, and I was close to one of them, whose name was Jane, a very creative individual. Her house was so well decorated by her own creativity. She used to be my walking buddy. One day as I walked passed her house; I saw her sitting with a man in the front seat of a Cadillac ready to drive away. She waved at me so I moved on and walked away. Next day she appeared at my door, and she was furious. I calmed her down, and asked her what was bothering her so much. She told me about her "date" with a man in his nineties. The man in the Cadillac that I saw the day before took her out to dinner. When they returned to her place, he asked her if she had heard of a disease called AIDS. At that point Jane got very upset and told him to leave immediately. I tried to humor her saying perhaps he had taken the medicine Viagra, and was thinking that time was running out on him, so take action quickly. My friend was not amused, because she felt very insulted by the guy's behavior, and I was still getting my culture shock that a 90 plus years old guy was going on a dinner date.

In the same community I had some German friends. I liked the Germans; I felt they were less pretentious, and very friendly. Sometimes I would join them for an afternoon coffee get together, called a coffee clutch. There I learnt so much about people, and found it very interesting. One guy was talking about how he spent time in Texas picking cotton. I asked him since you are German how did you pick cotton as a young man in Texas? He said he was fighting as a German soldier in Algeria in the WWII, and the Americans captured him and brought him to Texas as a P.O.W., where his job was to pick cotton. After he was sent back to Germany he later returned to the USA and made a very good life. I felt this is the USA with which we all fall in love, and want to settle here. I do not think prisoners taken by Russians would have gone back to live there after release, but that is my opinion.

In that community there were a few Chinese Americans married to white men. I did not have a chance to get to know them personally, but I really formed a very good opinion of these women. Chinese women in general have accomplished a lot in the USA in every field. They have advanced in television journalism, and I can name a few such journalists like glamorous Connie Chung, Ju Ju Chang, Julie Chen and Lucy Liu. I have referred to Liu's work earlier about a documentary she made about Indian child labor. Then there is fashion icon Vera Wang whose wedding gowns sell for many thousand dollars, and fashionable women want to be seen in a Vera Wang dress and at the Academy Award ceremony celebrities declare they are wearing a Vera Wang gown. I haven't read much about Chinese American literary work; only one book that I read was Joy Luck Club, by Amy Tan. This was a very interesting book which dealt with two generations of different nationalities coming together in the same household as a mother and a daughter. Then there are the trophy wives such as Mrs. Wendy Murdoch the many decades junior wife of Billionaire news media mogul, Rupert Murdoch. Then of course, every four years we get to watch pretty looking girls from China doing their best to nail down perfect scores in Gymnastics trying to beat the Europeans. They really have come a long way from the oppressions that they had gone through in the past. China and India are two huge countries with very old cultures. While Chinese culture remained pretty much secluded from influence by others and became regimented under Communism, Indian Culture got mixed up with Muslim culture and then with the British. Now India is trying to move ahead in a mixed culture in a secular democracy. This year they are celebrating 60 years of their freedom, but they have to be strong to handle the sectarian fundamentalism that is very much evident in that part of the world.

My Friend Pushpa

I started taking a few trips within the country and as well as abroad, and it was possible because I found a very good dog sitter for my TimTim. She was my hair stylist. She loved Timmy and Timmy was very fond of her. One of those trips was to New York to visit my friend Pushpa. She and her husband Arun are dear friends of mine and were excellent hosts, though they are much younger than I. All three of us were born and brought up in Varanasi. Pusphpa and I made our lives in the USA. She got married and her husband helped her to raise the family. He also got his doctorate degree in the USA. They both held important positions in industry.

I knew Puspha as a little girl, her father was a colleague of mine, and whenever I visited him he spoke very fondly of his daughter. Also, he talked about her brilliance in Mathematics and Sciences. I had lost track of them after I left India. Years later I met her, at a scientific meeting in Washington DC, where she was attending the meeting as Dr. Pushpa. I was very pleasantly surprised to meet her and learnt that she and her husband Arun were living in Princeton, NJ. I had a very good visit with her, and I was quite impressed to know of her achievements. I thought it would be worthwhile to write about her here.

She had attended the same High school in Varanasi as I did. Since the Washington DC meeting, we kept in touch and later I met her husband Arun, who had finished his PhD degree. I visited them several times, and we also vacationed together. They were excellent hosts. I remember visiting the New England states with them covering many hundreds of miles through the beautiful country side. At the far eastern shore of Maine in the little town of Kennebunkport, we saw Sr. Bush's summer residence; it was such a sight. At the time he was the President. I even sent some picture post cards from there to my Republican friends in California suggesting that he should retire to live in that beautiful place. He was defeated and Mr. Clinton became the next President.

In one of my visits, I sat down to learn more about Pushpa's life. It deserves to be written up in some magazine so that young women get inspiration and directional pointers in their life pursuits of academic achievements. A summarized account follows.

After finishing her Higher Secondary at the top of the class she obtained her B.Sc and Ms. Degrees in physical sciences and chemistry, respectively from Varanasi, as usual at the top of the class. After that she was admitted to the graduate school with full scholarship in Chemistry at the University of British Columbia, Vancouver, Canada. At the time she was only 21 years old and had led a sheltered life and never going very far from her hometown alone. At that University she completed her course requirements, but did not find the department challenging enough to continue there. Luckily, she had connections at MIT (Massachusetts Institute of Technology), Cambridge, USA, who suggested that she transfer her credentials from UBC to MIT. We know full well MIT, Harvard, Yale and Stanford are the best schools in the whole world. She went ahead and applied for admission and was accepted at MIT with a full scholarship so she moved to Cambridge, Mass., USA. As she was finishing her graduate work, her major professor who was an Englishman, decided to move back to Oxford University as the head of the department of Chemistry. She could have continued with another MIT professor but instead she decided to move to Oxford with the understanding that she would finish her research at Oxford but defend her thesis and graduate from MIT, Mass. It took her only three years to complete her degree, which was remarkable. She stayed at Oxford for one more year on one condition that her professor would help her to get a position with a reputable pharmaceutical company, preferably in the USA. Her research specialty was in antibiotics. Her professor kept his part of the bargain and wrote highly recommended letters to six companies in the U.S. It was also arranged in such a way that all six would interview her about the same time such that she did not have to travel several times between London and USA for interviews. Two companies selected her and she decided to join Squibb at Princeton, which was a fortuitous move on her part. Also, it is worth mentioning that at the time she was the only woman with a PhD degree at that company.

Pushpa as I understand did not have any kind of hobby and sort of stayed aloof. She expressed her desire to her mother in India that she wanted to get married in the old-fashion way. Her mother found her a husband, who was a friend of one of her son's. They were happily married and have a good life together. She stayed with the same company and advanced to Associate Director's position and after five years she became Executive director, her current position with 70 people working under her. Her meteoric rise was not a hindrance in her family life, and she became the mother of two children a girl and a boy, who are doing very well scholastically.

She is still a few years from retirement, so I expect her to advance in the company to a Vice President's position as she works hard. I have seen her work hard. Her husband gives her a helping hand with the family. I am impressed by her achievements; she demonstrated determination and good judgment as she was going through her young life all by herself in a far away land. I wish her all the best. Now, she and her husband derive satisfaction in their children's achievements. I could write about her scientific and production capabilities from start to finish, but I will let her tell about her life. I feel good though, because I have written about another Varanasi woman.

Our Trip to France

On one of my trips I went to France with my friend Linda and her daughter Amanda. Amanda was completing some course work at Dijon, France. It was a very enjoyable trip for the three of us. I had been to Paris several times but I had never seen the French country side, so I decided to join Linda and visit France and by- pass Paris, and I am glad I did. It was the most enjoyable trip that I had taken lately. Amanda was already there and awaiting our arrival, we met her at Paris Charles Degaulle Airport. At the airport I noticed some Tamil-looking Indians working and I realized that must be France's Pondicherry connection. Pondicherry used to be a French colony in India.

Linda rented a car, and she drove through the French country side to Dijon, which is famous for its mustard. We stayed there for a few days in a small but very comfortable hotel and enjoyed just relaxing. One evening we went to the Opera, which was a gift to us from Amanda. From there, we went to south-eastern France to a place called Baune, which was a quaint little town, there we visited a sprawling hospital-like set up to demonstrate how nursing was done as a profession as early as1400 AD, to take care of veterans without families who had fought in France's Hundred year war which started in 1337. It was the longest fought war in history between England and France. There was room after room like in a hospital setting, where mannequin nurses and patients were arranged in different positions, also, the kitchen and the make believe food were displayed so well, as if in a hospital dining area. No wonder in a recent WHO (World Health Organization) report France was the at top of the list of more than one hundred countries, for best in patient care in the world. France pays attention to the medical needs of its people. We also saw first hand, how the French medical system works when Linda needed medical attention for her discomfort, and needed immediate attention. Our hotel gave her a doctor's name, and she got an appointment immediately by telephone. She was examined by the doctor and he gave her a prescription for the antibiotic. We went to the neighborhood Apothecary (drug store) and got her prescription filled. The total cost, doctor and medicine was about $50. In the U.S., one has to go to an Emergency doctor and wait for a long time before seeing the doctor, and the same medicine would have cost her close to $100, and who knows the amount of the doctor's charge? They are not even set up to accept the cash payments, if there is no insurance involved. From Baune we drove east to the mountainous town of Annecy, by a beautiful Alpine lake in the neighboring Switzerland. The town is well connected by canals similar to Venice and it is an artist's community. From there we drove through the beautiful Loire valley non- stop to Renne in the Brittany area where we visited one of the worlds' oldest cathedrals, a beautiful huge edifice. We also took a side trip to Quimper, famous for a special kind of pottery. Linda had a great time shopping. I bought a cup, which is in my cup-display cabinet. From there we drove to the Atlantic coastal town, Dinard, a scenic place, and Mont St. Michel; I don't think we saw the famous rock out of the water for which it is famous. From there we visited Bayeux, famous for its 1000 years- old tapestry collection hung non stop in the temperature controlled museum. It was beautiful, and French people know how to preserve their antiquity. We then drove to Omaha beach, Normandy. This was a very emotional visit for all three of us. Normandy stands testament to what these fallen heroes did to preserve good over evil. That was quite a time in history. Linda did an excellent job of driving through France, and figuring out the way. Of course, Amanda was a great help to her. We met some local French people who were so polite, and who appreciated Linda and Amanda for their knowledge of French which for me was a small inconvenience, because France is a big beef eating country. The coastal towns were ok, because I could eat seafood. From there we drove to Versailles and visited the palace, which is one of the best in the world. We arrived in Paris, and I said good bye to Linda and Amanda and left by train to Germany to visit my sister. It was a four hour trip by a train which was very comfortable, safe and top of the line. I do not know why we do not have such good service in the USA. Of course, I am not including India here. They have a long way to go.

When I returned from Germany I joined Linda at a hotel near the airport, and left Paris next morning. This was one of my best vacations. Linda and Amanda were two very good companions to travel with, and I am looking forward to my visit to Florence, Italy to attend Amanda's wedding and spending some time in that neighborhood with Linda and her husband Richard.

My Next Residence Move

A number of my neighbor-friends were moving out of our neighborhood for various reasons. Some were moving to be near their children, or moving to relocate in a care- home, where they did not have to do household chores, in short the American society is very mobile. In that paradigm, I also moved around. One day, I read in my newspaper that a community similar to the one in which I was living advertised some of those newly built homes providing new refrigerators and washer dryers. I was curious, because my appliances were getting old and needed replacement as I decided to look into it. As usual, there was an 800 telephone number and I called and was connected with a lady who was a savvy business- woman, a sales person with the construction company. She helped me to make up my mind to buy one of those new homes in that community. This was also a gated community for adults 55 or older. I traveled 90- 100 miles round trip to visit the site and to sign papers for the sale and to take care of many things involved in that sale including the financing of the property. I thought I did well. My next step was to sell my house. I listed it for sale with a Real Estate company and I was anticipating a good price, because my house had appreciated in the last three years. The Real Estate lady was quite good, and I hoped for it to sell quickly. My sister came from Germany to give me a helping hand in my move and she started packing my China and Crystal etc. She also visited the property several times with me. Many prospective buyers walked through my house, and my sister and I would go away while they looked at the house. My doggie, Timmy had the worst time, because I had to chain him in the garage every time a prospective buyer came.

This was also the time that I lost my long friendship with Barbara (Mrs. D). This lady was becoming a little psychotic calling me frequently to tell me that her ex husband was coming to visit her along with a young woman and a child. As far as I knew her ex was nowhere near that town, and he was rather old to walk around with a little child. Many times I had to tell her that I was going to leave the house and that I will call her back, but she had the impression that I was avoiding her, and was upset. I really wanted to visit with her to try to get some medical help for her. I had my own problems to tackle, and also she lived 3000 miles away. I felt sad, because she was a dear friend, and I had had some very good times with her. Before I close this chapter of my life I wanted to know about her, therefore I decided to get in touch with her sister Marlene, whom I also knew very well. She was her only sister and a pragmatic individual who did not dwell in the dreamland like her sister. Luckily I had her telephone number, and when I called her she answered the phone. I told her who I was and she sounded very happy to hear from me. Her first question was "where have you been, you were the only bright spot in Barbara's life". Then I felt better so I asked her about Barbara. I told her that I lost contact with Barbara, now that I am writing a book I wanted to know about her. She told me that a few years ago she became very sick so she decided to go there and give her a helping hand (I presumed it was at the time when I felt she was becoming psychotic) and she admitted her in a nursing home. She then realized that her husband never visited her, therefore, she went looking for him. To her surprise she found him on the floor, without clothes, dead. She rose to the occasion and took care of that much unexpected situation. She then decided to bring her sister to Tennessee near her. She was placed in a home-care facility, where her mother was also taken care of. It was easy that way for Marlene to take care of both. Her mother passed away last November, since then Barbara is left alone there. She is now wheel chair bound, suffers from dementia and diabetes. I was not quite surprised to learn all that, my memory went back to the day when I had met her at the rooming house, and we became close friends. I thanked Marlene for all that information, and then I asked her how she was doing? She said in addition to all this stressful life she suffered from colon cancer, which is now in remission, and undergoing routine check-up regularly. She was very thankful to her husband who gave her all the support that she needed. Her children are all doing fine. She invited me to visit her in Tennessee.

My sister returned to Germany, and I also had an offer on my house. I was now packing at full speed to move out of the place, and my new house was almost ready. I had already finished the final "Walk through" of the new house to look and report to the Builder any problem that the house may have. I had already lined up a moving company to move to the new place. I had advertised to sell my appliances, and one day a young white couple stopped by who wanted to buy them, so I sold them at a reasonable price. The young woman noticed that my house was still not packed up ready to move, so she offered her help, and said she would tidy up the place after my house was moved. I did not see any problem and said alright. One day, I stepped out for 10 minutes to pick up some ice from the neighbor's, and after the day's work, I let the woman leave. I was ready to go out to dinner when I noticed that my diamond ring was missing. I had a sinking feeling that the ring was stolen by my handy- woman. Next day when she came to work, I told her about my ring but she would not admit it. I felt sad loosing the ring. Because it was one of my proud possessions, and I had purchased it with the money I received from my first tax return. Despite careful guarding every thing comes to an end and I lost my ring. I did report to the Police about the theft and to my Insurance Company from whom I did recover some money back.

I had scheduled the Movers to move my household on a Saturday, and on Friday I was still putting things together in my bed room when suddenly I started to have a severe stomach ache, which compelled me to drive my car to a hospital emergency where I thought I would ask them to give me the "green Cocktail" which had worked before. At the emergency, I did have the "cocktail" but it did not help me, and I was in excruciating pain. Finally, they gave me a heavy duty pain killer that helped me. Eventually, the Dr. arrived and he gave me news that I was not ready for. He said I should undergo gall-bladder surgery immediately and that, if I do not then I would have a bigger problem than I could handle. I wanted to go home and take care of my moving and then schedule my surgery and he said no to that. I was admitted for surgery immediately, and I discussed with the Anesthesiologist about my sensitivity to some anesthetics but, he said that since my episode 30 years ago, things have advanced very much and I should be all right with that I said my mantra and tried to get ready for the surgery. I used my cell phone to call Barbara to ask her to take care of Timmy who was left alone at the house so Mark, Barbara's husband put the doggie in a kennel. I also called my real estate lady to say that I would not be able to vacate the house as planned, and every thing has to be "on hold" until later. This lady did not accept my decision and instead she took over the situation and decided to move any way since she had my house keys.

That Saturday, instead of moving to my new house, I was getting ready for my surgery. Every thing was moving so rapidly that I did not get a chance to inform any body including my sister in Germany. In this day and age with the telephone system every where, the news was disseminated quickly. I was in the process of moving, and my realtor lady who was in my house putting things together helping the movers, answered a call on my telephone, and an Indian-Tamil friend, Enid who was just trying a social call from far away Kansas State, learnt that I was undergoing surgery. She was so worried that she called my other Indian-Tamil friends Raj and Hildah. Soon every body got to know that I was having surgery, including my sister and then they started calling the hospital, there I was going through the same scenario as I did several decades ago reacting to anesthetics from which I almost died. I do not know the whole story because I was comatose for about 48 hours post surgery. However, I was given to understand that Raj's daughter, who is a nurse in LA at the same hospital but not aware of my first episode, where I had had the same reaction many years ago, gave directions to the Anesthesiologist on what to do. After a few days of struggle as a recovering patient, I came through the ordeal and went to recover at Barbara's for about 10 days or so.

To My New House

After I recovered and rested for quite a few days, Barbara drove me to my new house and I was happy to see that the realtor lady did a good job moving my house hold and arranging the furniture such that I did not have to move any thing again. My job now was to open those boxes which were piled up in the garage. Barbara offered to help, and she arranged the kitchen. Next day I went to the kennel to pick up Timmy. As soon as he saw my car he started barking to beat the band. I first went to the office to pay my bill and to retrieve the doggie. He was so happy to see me and so was I. It took him some time to get used to the new house and the new environment; but he adjusted quickly.

I was also helped to open boxes and arrange things at my new place by some other friends who had dropped by to see my new property. I remember that my friends Horst and Elle helped hang the pictures and arranged books and knick-knacks. My next order of business was to fix the back yard, which was just a vast open land. Soon I started calling to find landscape developer, and settled on one which the others were also hiring. It took him a few weeks to get started. He gave me a blue print of the job he was going to do which was a $25,000 job. My back yard is probably the largest in the neighborhood, and my neighbors say it looks like a park. I like to work in my backyard.

I got to know my new neighbors, who are all friendly retired people, age 55 and older including the couple who lived opposite. The lady was in her 80's and her husband was in his 70's. She was called Boot's, her nick name, a very beautiful woman, who dressed exquisitely. At the club house restaurant, people would come to her and ask if she was a movie actress. She looked and dressed like one of those stars such as Ava Gardner, Lana Turner and so on. Ed was her second husband, a very prim and proper gentle-man. Whenever I met him out side he would be extremely polite and exchanged pleasantries. Boots on the other hand would complain about him, she would come down to have tea with me which she enjoyed. She started telling me that Ed wanted to institutionalize her, because she was loosing her marbles. They went to a Neurologist, who diagnosed her as old age loosing her memory, nothing serious. Then she asked me to find her a divorce attorney. She wanted to go to an attorney without Ed. I found an attorney and she got an appointment, to which I was to drive but she changed her mind and did not go to the attorney after all. I got the impression that Ed realized that this time her complaint may hold so he made up with her. Within a short time Ed had a stroke and he did recover, but not fully. One day as I drove home I noticed he was lying on their drive way, and Boots was sitting next to him on a chair. I parked my car and walked up to the couple and asked what was happening. Ed spoke up and said that he fell, but I would not be able to help him, because he was a heavy set man. As I was debating in my mind if I should call 911 for help I noticed a car slowed and the driver shouted "do you people need help"? I said yes, then the man came and helped Ed get up. As usual, he was very polite and thanked us profusely, and we left. Within a few days his end came, and he was gone. As per his wish he was cremated, and there was no funeral service, so I gathered all the neighbors, who knew Ed at my house and arranged a mini-memorial service and provided some food to serve. I told them to say something good about Ed, and also to give me in writing whatever was said. It worked out well; I gathered all those writings and sent them to Boots, who was then in Alabama. I think she appreciated that. We neighbors helped Boots cope with the situation prior to her departure. Her neighbors were very helpful to her. Her niece and her husband came from Alabama and took her back with them. She used to call me from Alabama, her new place. She turned 90, and still in good health, but I could see that she was deteriorating by her telephone conversations, repeating several times the same thing she was saying. One day she called, and I was busy with some thing so I told her I would call her back, but within a couple of days she had died. I knew Boots only for three years, but she was a unique woman. She once told me her background and that she left Alabama at age 18 to go west to California looking for a better life which she found. She was a jewelry designer, and I used to wonder how we all converged in California for a better life.

I must write about my friend from Texas, Albina who lives on the other side of this neighborhood and who is a single lady, having lost her husband a few years ago. She is a very benevolent and giving person who helps her neighbors all the time. I appreciated her help also, without which my writing on this laptop computer would be impossible. Whenever I had computer technical difficulty she was there to get me through. She is a computer savvy great- grandmother.

I wanted to say thank you to all my friends who had come and helped me out, so I decided to celebrate my birthday and invited a lot of friends. I went ahead and rented one of the three club houses, and I had the food catered. Just a few days before the get-together I had one of the worst days of my life. Timmy, my doggy, who was not quite 14, yet was sick. One day he just could not get up, so I called the veterinarian and he came and examined him and felt a big lump in his abdominal area. He suggested x-ray, blood test etc. and I sent doggy with him, because Timmy needed help to get there. I knew that was the end of my doggie because he had a tumor, and needed surgery so I decided instead of the surgical trauma to let Timmy go. That was very depressing for me; Barbara came by and visited with me for a while. I talked to my sister, who loved my doggie very much and told me do not put him to sleep until she arrived, but she arrived a few days later. Therefore, the party turned out to be very good therapy for me. My sister attended, so did Om and Indira from Texas and many friends in southern California. I thanked them one by one chronologically as they appeared in my life, for coming. We had a wonderful time and a special thanks to Barbara who did the table decorations and provided the birthday cake.

I gave myself a traveling gift to travel to the Adriatic coast for a two week visit. My itinerary consisted of a visit to the fortified wall city and Minceta tower of Dubrovnik. We went sightseeing on a walking tour of the Pile Gate, Franciscan Monastery and St. Blaise Church and Clock Tower. In the evening we had dinner hosted by a local family, which we appreciated very much and we attended a Classical Music concert at St. Savior's Church. From there we departed for a place called Split. There we took a walking tour with visits to Diocleatian Palace including Peristyle Square, Cathedral St. Dominus, and Temple of Jupiter etc. Then we traveled to Sibenik, for Karka National Park for a panoramic tour of the area. We departed for an unspoiled Dalmatian village a relic of the past in this Mediterranean coast and then to Opatija, the resort town on the Adriatic Riviera. From there we went inland to Zagreb via Plitvice Lakes, where we did some boating. Croatia's capital Zagreb is a picturesque little town and we enjoyed a concert at the National Theater. We then took a side tour to Lake Bled in Slovenia by way of Ljubljana. This beautiful little scenic place is nestled against Slovenia's Julian Alps and used to be a play ground of the rich and famous, now of course every kind of tourist is seen. We returned to Zagreb to take our flight back home. I enjoyed very much that Adriatic trip, National Geographic Adventure declared Croatia as "the paradise on earth" and I felt there is some truth to it.

Next year I took a trip to Kolkata, India and I enjoyed myself very much visiting my cousins and their families. My cousin Pintu took time to show me and my sister how that city had improved. I thank him for that, but I felt that whatever improvement they made does not make a dent because of the population which is increasing so much. I did see a lot more cell phones and they are talking nonstop oblivious of place or who is around. I also felt there were more vehicles on the roads. I visited the house of Rabindra Nath Tagore, Nobel laureate in literature, and was disappointed. It was a huge house but there was nothing to show in the rooms any where. This man did not live austere like his contemporary national figure Mahatma Gandhi in loin cloth; Tagore was a fashionable man and lived in style. In the USA such a house will be full of memorabilia and in Bonn, Germany I saw Beethoven's house which was full of his belongings arranged every where as if he was still living there. I also visited an orphanage and donated some cash and good will from my American friends. The saintly man, in charge of the place showed us around as little boys went about living their lives. I believe they need this kind of operation a lot more, and I do not know if they have such similar orphanages for females.

My trip to Florence, Italy

As I returned from Florence after attending Amanda's (Linda's daughter) wedding, I noticed there were quite a few messages left on my telephone including two messages left by Cyndi, Martha's daughter. I had strange feelings about those calls, therefore, I went ahead and called Cyndi right away and learned that her mother, my dear friend Martha had passed away while I was on my trip. As I wrote earlier that she was ailing, and was bed ridden, I was not surprised to know of her passing. However, death is always hard to accept, especially as she was so dear to me. I remembered that as a young woman, along with her husband, she came to pick me up for my first Thanksgiving holiday, and now she was gone. I told Cyndi that I share her grief and I shall get in touch with her soon.

My trip to Florence started quite a few days later when Linda arrived from the bay area. Next day she drove back with me and the day after Linda, Richard and I took our flight to Chicago from San Francisco. Our first stop was Chicago then on the way to Heathrow, London. These two airports are the world's largest and as chaotic as it comes, compounded by the terrorist scare. I appreciated all the security measures, though there may be loop-holes through which the evil-doers could pull function, but so far security measures are holding, and we boarded the planes without the terrorist worries. At London-Heathrow we had a four hours wait for the next flight. These big airports have taken advantage by bringing the fancy shopping to waiting passengers. My friend Linda, who loves shopping, wanted to visit Harrods which was nearby. She found a good buy and bought a Farragamo hand bag for $400, the initial price was $800. We then took a Lufthansa flight to Munich, Germany. After waiting in Munich for a few hours we were told at the boarding time that the Lufthansa flight was suddenly cancelled because they determined that there were flight hazards with the Bombardier-8 planes. These planes, made in Canada were in the news about some defects. After negotiating with them for quite a while, we were routed via Rome, Pisa by Italian airlines, Alitalia, and finally to Florence by ground travel. The plane in Rome was a propeller –plane, which required a long runway to take off. We all felt it was the most hazardous flight so far. We finally arrived at the hotel at 2am without our suitcases, which did not arrive. We were exhausted and retired for whatever was left of the night. Our bags arrived three days later.

This Florence wedding was in the making shortly after Amanda became engaged to Michael on Valentine's Day in 2006. Since when she started planning marriage. She found a marriage coordinator in Florence, Italy on the internet who arranged every detail about the marriage. The wedding took place in Palazzo Vechio, an ancient huge building in its matrimonial hall. A city council woman appointed by the Mayor with the authority to perform the matrimony performed the marriage of Amanda and Michael in a civil ceremony. Amanda through her coordinator had hired an interpreter, and they said their vows in English. In the background soft music played on the Harp. It was a small wedding party with a bride's maid and the best man and a few relative and friends attending. The bridegroom's 85 years old grandma, universally called Nana also attended the wedding. Amanda wore a beautiful custom made wedding gown, and she looked beautiful. She was helped with her hair and make up by a local beautician. Michael also looked very handsome in a tuxedo. The usual wedding pictures were taken done by a professional photographer and the ceremony lasted less than an hour.

In the evening we went for a seven course wedding dinner at a local restaurant called Il Celestino where white, red wine and champagne were served with the dinner. The wedding cake was a multi layered Italian cake, which was excellent. We left for our hotel about mid night. I was sharing my hotel room with the bridesmaid, Julie and that night instead of her returning to the room; Amanda came in looking for something. What I understood from her was Julie's foot got caught up in the revolving entry way and got badly injured with massive bleeding. She was rushed to the Emergency, where she was taken care of and given four stitches and then she returned to her room. Her emergency care was without any charge. Next day Amanda and Michael left on their honeymoon to Greece and Turkey.

Richard, Linda and I stayed on for a few more days and visited the nearby little town of Fiesola which is on top of the rolling hills overlooking the valley There was an amphitheater, which was ancient, but not in a ruinous condition. Then there was a museum, which also had many priceless paintings, but this place was not as big as Uffizi in Florence, which we had visited the day before. At this place we saw most ancient remains dating back to second millennium B.C. including artifacts from Bronze age, the Iron Age and the Archaic Etruscan Age. The Uffizi or "offices" was built in mid 16th century to hold all the administrative offices, however later it was turned into an art gallery and museum. There were three corridors and 45 rooms. In the corridors classical sculptures and statues were located and the paintings were hung in different rooms. In order to appreciate this massive collection of paintings and art memorabilia, one has to spend quite a few days in this building. But we just touched bases by rushing through the corridors and a few rooms. Some of the works of art by such familiar names like Botticelli, Leonardo Da Vinci, Michelangelo, Raphael, Rembrandt and many others were very well represented. I was amazed how these people have preserved all these hundreds- of-years -old art work over the years through many centuries maintaining their originality.

We left Italy for London via Frankfurt and we spent one night in London and next day returned back to the USA. It was good to be back home.

Epilogue

I decided to write about my life based on my memory, which I felt at times as if I am writing about something that had happened just yesterday. Though sometimes my senior moments "will" erase the present happenings, the past had been preserved well. I must say I enjoyed writing, because I found I had inner strength supported by tools that helped me through my life, considering what my beginning was.

Through this writing I wanted to express my appreciation especially to my mother and grand mother. I felt their sacrifices helped me to grow and develop my thinking differently from theirs. Even though I did not like living in a far away land from my family, I like the over all outcome because I could see the variations in our life styles and how Indian women came out in modern times. I also felt a connection with the world which I would not have had if I stayed in India. In the broader context when I can get along with people from different backgrounds why can't countries get along? My recent trip gave me the impression that countries fear individuals who have taken upon themselves the terrorist activities to destroy whatever does not conform to their religious beliefs and way of life. As my plane was landing in Heathrow-London airport, I could see that huge city and how it is attractive to the terrorists to create mischief. I felt with the advancing technology, they can even zero in on a site to attack, but I also felt Londoners have done a very good job in controlling the huge numbers of passengers going through their doors. Then there is Italy, the country that appears to me to consist of many art galleries and museums. Every where I went I saw paintings and sculptures adorning the walls and corridors.

From the USA I could see why Indian women are looked at in a stereotypical way by the West, though there are so many accomplished Indian women at the top of their field. But it is the masses that get written up in newspapers and magazines. It is the Indian women as laborers carrying loads of bricks or whatever and without properly clothed that are photographed and written up. My complaint is why the builders and industrialists do not make attempts to better the lives of these people. India now has a Madam-President and I hope she will facilitate some of these changes.

I have also seen some of the environmental abuses in India, and I feel as if the people, who could make a difference, do not care. In one of my visit to the Indian financial capital, Bombay I found the Arabian Sea contaminated with all kinds of debris including plastic baggies floating around giving a very shabby look right around the famous Taj-Mahal hotel. Then in Kolkata while shopping in a modern building housing a shopping center I noticed a wall covered with red betel-nut juice spit in a massive way. I approached a few shop-owners and suggested to put up a camera and record the people who are defacing such buildings and penalize them with a big monetary fine or some sort of punishment. They have to be strict in handing down punishments. My suggestion is the city administrator should make a trip to neighboring Singapore and learn how to clean up.

I do hope that modern India which is doing well also should spruce up the country; it just needs some will- power to bring in such changes. And finally women, they have to move into the twenty first century in every aspect in life, including physical activity. Most common diseases in women such as Osteoporosis (bone-thinning), diabetes, hypertension, breast cancer etc can be controlled by proper nutrition and physical activity. They can be reached by television programs, newspaper writings and such modern mode of communication "internet". For instance Breast-cancer support group is very active in the West on internet. But in India and Muslim countries it is a taboo to talk about woman's heath, leave aside Breast cancer.

In its recent annual report by the Swiss-based World Economic Forum in which 128 countries were ranked on the basis of gender equality. The report measures the discrepancies between men and women in four categories: 1. Educational attainment 2. Economic participation and opportunity 3. Political empowerment 4. Health and survival (Time 2007).

India is in the bottom 15 countries. That is a shame.

As I was about to end my writing I received a newspaper article from my friend Anita that she read in her local paper "The Californian", and she thought I should see it. The article is about a documentary named "white Rainbow" made by an Indian film maker, Dharan Mandayar. Through his film he focused on the abuse of widows that still exists in India. So far he has not been successful in showing the film to the North Indians. I know the kind of abuse a widow goes through is generally carried out by women, under the tutelage of Manu of Manusmriti, a man. It has not changed since it was prescribed by him. I do not know how that can be changed, but the new woman President Patil should give serious consideration to effecting changes to enable women to assume a more active roll in modern day living. Finally, Indian men have to emerge in a big way strong enough to take the leadership for more than a billion people. Unfortunately, they are still influenced by the Nehru-Gandhi dynasty. No wonder Sonia Gandhi, an Italian born, naturalized Indian citizen plays such a leading roll in Indian politics.

*I must acknowledge some of my friends who have
been telling me to write my life story; they thought
I had a lot to tell. So here is my story.
I have bypassed parts of my working life, therefore is is
mostly the story of my family and friends. My very special
thanks to my friends John Lee and Raj Pakkinathan for
without their help this would not have been possible. John
for reading and editing my manuscript, and Raj for his help
with the computer. My thanks to my friends who helped me
in every way they could. My thanks to my sister, KumKum,
who gave me the names of the vegetation in our Grandma's
garden and also helped me to remember some occasions.
Lastly my thanks to Sheela Singla, who
had done the cover art work.*

gramcontent.com/pod-product-compliance
Source LLC
rg PA
280526
001BA/480